Two

Training for uncertainty

Library of Social Work

General Editor:
Noel Timms
Professor of Social Work Studies
University of Newcastle upon Tyne

Training for uncertainty
A sociological approach to social work education

Brian Heraud

Routledge & Kegan Paul
London, Boston and Henley

First published in 1981
by Routledge & Kegan Paul Ltd
39 Store Street, London WC1E 7DD,
9 Park Street, Boston, Mass. 02108, USA and
Broadway House, Newtown Road,
Henley-on-Thames, Oxon RG9 1EN
Printed in Great Britain by
Redwood Burn Ltd, Trowbridge, Wilts

British Library Cataloguing in Publication Data

Heraud, Brian
Training for uncertainty: a sociological
approach to social work education. – (Library
of social work)
1. Social work education
I. Title   II. Series
361.3'07   HV10.5

ISBN 0–7100–0889–9

Contents

Acknowledgments

Grateful acknowledgments are made for permission to reproduce material in this book. Table 4.1 has been reproduced by permission of the author and the Social Administration Research Trust of the London School of Economics. Table 5.1 has been reproduced by permission of the author and Routledge and Kegan Paul. Material from Tables 7.1 and 7.2 have been reproduced by permission of the authors, Basil Blackwell and the University of Exeter. Table 10.1 has been reproduced by permission of the author and the British Association of Social Workers.

I should like to thank the Open University for permission to use material from Professionalism in Social and Community Work in 'Social Work, Community Work and Society', Course DE206.

This work originated in a postgraduate degree thesis submitted to the University of London, and I should like to acknowledge a grant from the University of London Central Research Fund. I should like to acknowledge the help of all the social work students and teachers who were involved in the original research. I owe an especial debt to Professor Margot Jefferys for her supervision of the original work, and to Professor Noel Timms and Philippa Brewster for their help and encouragement in the preparation of this book. The help and support of Juliet Heraud during the period of the original work was invaluable. I should also like to thank Diane Porter for her help and encouragement and Audrey Brett for typing much of the manuscript.

Chapter one

Introduction

They tell us their aim is to change us; at the moment a
very strong feeling going around that not going to change
any of us. Quite a few of us who say we don't want to be
changed - want to develop our skills but don't want to be
changed. (1st Year social work student; Heraud, 1972)

In contemporary social work criticism and dissatisfaction
with social work education is matched by equally strong
defences, explanations and rationalisations of this type of
training. Intense debates surround issues such as the
purpose of training, the selection of students, the relationship between students and social work teachers, and the control of the curriculum and of assessment. Social work
education has not escaped the widespread wave of criticism
of most forms of professional practice that has been latent
for many years and which found particular expression
(mainly among students) in the 1960s and the early 1970s.
In reflecting on the present situation Donnison (1979) has
stated that:

I constantly come across past students ; ranging from last
year's graduates to married women returning to work 20
years after I last saw them in a lecture room - who are
bored and disillusioned by professional training. Whether
they intend to become social workers, town planners,
lawyers or teachers, far too many of them feel they are
undergoing a selection process to which they are compelled
to submit themselves, rather than a mind opening experience.

Such criticisms and controversies are in part a reflection of
the vast growth in professional training, particularly in
social work, in the years since the Second World War. The

numbers of students on courses of training which lead to a
professional social work qualification (CQSW) has risen from
98 in 1950 to over 3,700 in 1979 (Jones, 1964; CCETSW,
1980a). This has meant a considerable growth in the number
of social work teachers (both academic and fieldwork) and
departments and schools of social work in universities and
other institutions of higher education, as well as the centra-
lisation of the administration of the whole process, including
the validation of courses, in the form of the Central Council
for Education and Training in Social Work (CCETSW). The
budget of the Council increased from £383,000 in 1974 to
£1,300,000 in 1976-7 (Shearer, 1979). Such developments
represent what has been one of the most frequent responses
to the social problems of the 1960s, a call to produce more
social workers, although there are reasons for thinking
that this particular solution is now less likely to recommend
itself to governments and members of other professions.
Social work educators have shown considerable skill in
fostering such development, particularly in seeking voluntary and eventually state support for new ventures in training and in providing some of the necessary intellectual
leadership. Yet there has been little attempt to come to
grips with the meaning of such changes, or with the consequences both intended or unintended of them.

Certainly one issue that has constantly recurred is the
difficulty in defining the task of social work and the boun-
daries of practice. Without a solution to this problem it is
impossible, it is asserted, to devise an effective training
programme (Brewer and Lait, 1980). The alternative,
according to these authors, is to close most if not all training courses in favour of apprenticeship training while the
social work task is clarified. At another extreme, the
social work task appears clearer, with the implication that
social work education is to be defended, but both practice
and education must be challenged and changed because of
their irrelevance to the conflicts and contradictions which
social workers and their clients experience (Corrigan and
Leonard, 1978).

Such controversies have resulted in September 1980 in
the setting up of an official inquiry into social work and the
definition of the social work task, headed by the Chairman
of the National Institute of Social Work. Clearly, contemporary social work education is in a situation of considerable
uncertainty for teachers, students and administrators.
While uncertainty and the means of coping with this are a

necessary part of any training course, there is today a
heightened sense of uncertainty and conflict to which any
inquiry must give urgent attention.

While the arguments over social work education and practice have often taken on the extreme tones illustrated above,
many of the questions that can be asked in this area, and
which will form most of the content of this book, are basic
to any form of occupational education and training.

The class and ethnic background of social workers has for
long been a contentious subject and in the case of social
work students reflects the wider issue of the over representation of middle-class students in higher education generally.
The problem centres on the clash in perspective between
many social workers and their clients and relates to different
approaches to problem solving as well as to wider experiences of differing life chances, expectations and other class
based situations, such as long-term unemployment. It is
asserted that social work education gives a student little idea
of what it is like to be a client, and in fact often reinforces a
purely professional or bureaucratic definition of the client's
situation. Central to this controversy is the process of
selection of students for training, an issue which in recent
years has reached as far as the High Court. Class differences are also important in trying to assess the impact of
training on students – does the student with working-class
origins have an experience of training which is markedly
different from that of his middle-class contemporaries?

Social work teachers have also borne their share of criticism, particularly for their supposedly rather uncritical
attachment to an existing body of knowledge enshrined in the
course curriculum, their reluctance to develop new knowledge through research and their distance from the practical
skills that they profess. It is sometimes pointed out that
new knowledge of relevance to social work is generated
mainly outside the profession and the schools and departments
of social work training (Donnison, 1979). Against this it is
argued that social work knowledge is developing rapidly and
that social work teachers have played their part in this, although they also carry an unusually heavy burden of teaching,
tutorial and supervisory commitments and that their concern
must be given equally to students as to research. Yet the
role and status of academic and fieldwork teachers is clearly
one of considerable controversy and conflict.

The educational process in which social work teachers and
students are concerned involves problems which are found in

other forms of professional training; however in social
work one model of the educational process involves a particularly close teacher–student relationship in which the line
between academic and non–academic considerations is sometimes blurred.   Forms of assessment such as continuous
assessment also play their part in this situation.   There is
also the issue of the different and sometimes conflicting
models represented by the academic and fieldwork teacher,
and the problems of identification that this raises for students who may have very differing levels of academic and
practical experience.

One problem is certainly that of the entry of individuals,
often in adult life, into institutions which are involved not
only in education and training in a general sense, but with
the process of changing people.   The dilemma of the student
who is exposed to this, and to the tensions between the different elements of the training process, is well illustrated
by the epigraph to this chapter, and will be a major focus for
discussion in the book as a whole.

Student assessment has recently assumed even greater
importance not only because of the difficulty surrounding the
definition of professional standards and their attainment,
but because of the differing and sometimes conflicting principles involved.   One potential conflict is between the
assessment 'process' (concern for the educational and professional development of the student over time) and the
assessment 'event', whereby a student is assessed at a particular point in time,and the emphasis placed on the former
by some social work teachers.   This is seen as a potential
dilution in standards of professional knowledge and skill
attained by students at the end of their course (Brandon and
Davies, 1979).

STRUCTURE OF THE BOOK

This book is primarily concerned with professional education
and training in social work and with the important and con-
troversial issues surrounding this process today.   The main
focus of the book is on the structure of the socialising process, including the characteristics of teaching staff and
students, and the processes in which staff and students are
involved, such as role playing and the development of professional identity.   These themes are however treated socio-
logically in the sense that the discussion is grounded in

theoretical and conceptual approaches that sociologists have taken to the study of education and training in the professions (or 'professional socialisation').

The work originated in research for a higher-degree thesis which involved a longitudinal study of two groups of social work students in different educational settings (a university and a technical college), and which was also based upon theoretical approaches to the material generated by the research (Heraud, 1972). Staff and students were interviewed at different points in time and documentary information was collected about each course. For the purpose of this book the discussion of social work education has been updated and as much new material used as possible. While the original research is over ten years old, in which time there have been many changes in British social work, reference will still be made to this, and the original work will provide a framework for the book as a whole.

The colleges, courses and students of the original research will be referred to as the 'research colleges', 'research courses' and 'research students' throughout to distinguish them from other research which has been used. The two educational settings (which remain anonymous) will be referred to as the 'research university' and the 'research tech'. In the former the course was of a one year postgraduate nature and in the latter a two year non-graduate course. In both cases, successful completion of the course led to a professional qualification in social work. The courses were not intended to be representative of their type and the intention was analysis in depth. However the characteristics of the research students are very similar to those of all students on similar courses when comparisons are made (see chapter 7 for such comparisons).

In the years since this small pilot study there has been growing interest in research on social work education. This has varied from studies of individual courses in depth to more general studies of larger samples of students and their teachers in such areas as general attitudes to the quality and relevance of training and the nature of the assessment process by which the competence of students is determined. At the same time there have been a number of studies of the training process in other professions (notably teaching and health visiting; Lacey, 1977; and Dingwall, 1977) which have had a specifically sociological focus; it is the approaches and general orientation of studies such as these that have informed this book and to which it is hoped to make a contribution.

Chapter two

Professionalism and professional education

(1) STATUS PROFESSIONALISM

Education and training for the professions are a key feature of their contemporary organisation and their claims to status and reward in the occupational system. More than this, the specialised knowledge claimed by the professions and the way in which this is passed on through training has come to symbolise such claims. Such knowledge is also a matter of growing controversy and is part of the contemporary conflict between the professions, their clients and their critics.

But in the history of the professions, systems of education and training are of quite recent origin. Prior to the emergence of modern professionalism, which occurred in both Britain and the United States during a period covering little over two generations in mid nineteenth century (Larson, 1977), education and training for the professions was bound up with the elite status of such occupations. Until nineteenth-century industrialisation and its extended division of labour, the professions (mainly the church, medicine and the law) were not of primary importance in the general organisation of work (Elliott, 1972). While each profession claimed a certain responsibility for some area of work, this was often of less importance than the cultured, leisurely and gentlemanly existence to which this claim gave rise.

Professions and their members were able to claim a high status in society on social rather than functional grounds, and could hand this status on to those who could demonstrate an affinity with the style of life that was characteristic of such professions. These so called 'status professions' (ibid.) were linked to the highest levels of social status by the patronage of the aristocracy and landed gentry and depended on the power and prestige of such groups and the tightly knit community they represented for their own social position.

The key element which characterised the preparation of members of the status professions for their role was that of a classical and liberal education, an education fit for gentlemen and based upon a study of the classics and associated particularly with the public schools and the universities. This was education that confirmed a status which already existed and which related to an esteemed way of life, rather than to the possession of particular forms of knowledge and skill. The bare rudiments of the knowledge that was necessary for practice could be achieved through the initiative of the practitioner in the period following formal education. For example, medical knowledge could be obtained by 'walking the wards' of a London voluntary hospital, or by attending private medical schools. Until the nineteenth century, apart from certain financial provisions, attendance at the Inns of Court was the sole prerequisite for entry to the senior branch of the legal profession. The classical rather than technical education of the leading medical elite, the physicians, was defended on the grounds that it would make the latter more acceptable in the great houses of the aristocracy and the upper classes; without a veneer of classical learning it was felt that they would be at a loss in such company and this form of education insured that entrants to such an elite had the correct social background (Holloway, 1964). The intensive competitive climate of the professions, which would act as a discouragement to the incompetent, was often cited as a defence of the lack of specialised educational preparation for practice.

(2) THE CHALLENGE OF OCCUPATIONAL PROFESSIONALISM

The situation that has been described underwent a considerable change during the nineteenth century, although some of the relevant changes had their origin in a much earlier period. For example, secularisation had begun to free the professions from an educational system dominated by religious belief. Industrialisation was also changing the significance of the occupation an individual followed; previously the work a man or woman had performed had little importance

as an indicator of their social status, particularly for elite
status groups for whom work (even of a professional variety)
was deemed irrelevant for the purposes of ascribing status.
But in societies which were experiencing rapid social and
industrial change, the occupation an individual followed had
much greater significance; for this reason, as well as the
rapid expansion of scientific knowledge, occupational knowledge and expertise came to have a new and enhanced meaning. Thus a new kind of professionalism – occupational
professionalism based upon specialisation of knowledge and
task rather than the claim to a prestigious social position
alone – has arisen as a dominant form within the modern
occupational system (Elliott, 1972).

The existing elite of status professions had already experienced the challenge of related occupational groups of more
modest status, particularly the lower levels of the medical
and legal professions, including the surgeons, apothecaries
and attorneys. In medicine while there were internal conflicts among existing specialities, the needs of the new
middle classes for medical treatment were an important
factor in the promotion of new groups who, among other
things, were more accessible than the existing medical
elites. The apothecaries and surgeon apothecaries, who
had for some time practised in the wider community, were
able to answer such needs, and by the early nineteenth
century had come to be referred to as the 'general practitioners' of their day. A key to such developments was the
establishment of educational and qualifying arrangements
outside the existing formal structure of education. Such
qualifying associations (Millerson, 1964) stressed vocational
competence and the ability to pass examinations rather than
high social status and a classical education as the criteria
for entry to training and eventual licensing. This made
previously elite occupations more open to outside competition. In the context of contemporary criticism of examinations as the basis of professional qualification, it should be
noted that examinations were seen by nineteenth-century
reformers of the profession as the main element in their
attack on privileged and sponsored entry to the professions
and other elite institutions.

Another nineteenth-century development was the single
purpose professional training school, for example in the
army, the church and teaching. While such schools represented an attempt to codify and pass on a body of knowledge,
another interpretation of them is as a defensive response by

the established professions to what was seen as a threat to
their position.   The idea has re-emerged in contemporary
discussion of social work education, primarily as a defensive stratagem at a time of enhanced criricism (Davies,
1979).   While such schools symbolised the emergence of
occupational professionalism, they also incorporated elements from the past, particularly the desire to recruit
candidates with social characteristics thought desirable for
future membership of what were still social elites.   Thus
the systems of professional education that were emerging in
this period of rapid change contained two different educational ideals; to educate and train talented people for
specific professional tasks irrespective of social origins,
but also to confirm an existing social status by giving a professional training to the sons and daughters of existing
elites who already possessed a broad classical and liberal
education.   The tensions between these ideals has continued into the present day.   It is ironical, as Elliott (1972)
remarks, that the non-vocational liberal conception of education should have assumed such importance in a vocational
system and as a means of vocational advancement.   Because
access to this traditional form of knowledge was limited
through the hierarchy of existing educational institutions
(the public schools and universities) the introduction of competitive examination based entry, which was designed to
open up recruitment to the professions, had the effect of
formalising the connection between existing social elites and
the new occupational elites.

The universities were the basis of the liberal system of
education.   In an inaugural address to the University of St
Andrews, J.S. Mill sets down what he considered to be the
proper relationship between the universities' concern to
develop the 'whole man' and the occupational specialisation
which will follow, but not accompany it.   The university, he
argued (Rothblatt, 1968; cited in Elliott, 1972),

> is not a place of professional education.   Universities
> are not intended to teach the knowledge required to fit
> men for some special mode of gaining their livelihood.
> Their object is not to make skilful lawyers, or physicians,
> or engineers, but capable and cultivated human beings....
> Men are men before they are lawyers, or physicians or
> merchants, or manufacturers; and if you make them
> capable and sensible men, they will make themselves
> capable and sensible lawyers and physicians.

(3) PROFESSIONAL STRATEGIES

But the universities, apart from the liberal values they represented, were important in the situation facing the newly
emergent professions in their attempts to acquire a share of
new markets for their services, and in the development of
occupational professionalism.   As the markets for professional services began to expand, the task facing the newly
emergent professions was to give some form of guarantee of
the standard of the service that was being offered, other
than that afforded by the reputation and history of the profession.   As the professions offer, in the main, services
rather than actual commodities, the only way of guaranteeing
standards is by some basic mechanism for the production of
professionals, that is some form of socialisation procedure
by which such services can be offered and marketed.
Again if practitioners are to be educated they need some
form of guarantee that the sacrifices involved will be rewarded.   Professions will therefore attempt to obtain a monopoly over the services being offered (Larson, 1977).   But
the success or otherwise of such claims is not simply in the
hands of the professions themselves.   The market in which
a profession is operating and in which it is striving to have
the legitimacy of its claims accepted is influenced not only
by changing social needs and the attitudes of competing professions, but by wider social processes, particularly the
direction of social change in industrial societies.   Here a
debate exists between two sharply contrasting interpretations
of the place of the professions in industrial society and of the
key processes which are involved.
    Professions are, it is asserted (Oppenheimer, 1973),
little different from other occupations where bureaucratic
and managerial forms of authority determine the conditions of
work and the nature of the tasks to be performed.   In this
formulation the professions are, in the last analysis, not
much more resistant to this than other occupations.   The
consequence of this is that the professional is 'proletarian-
ised', and consequently is more likely to seek traditionally
working-class, trade union solutions to conflicts in the work
situation (such as strike action).   Professional training and
certification is not much more than a means of determining
advancement within this structure.   Another consequence is
that there is a considerable disjunction between the expectations built up through professional training and the actual
experience of work tasks which are fragmented and subject
to external control.

While there is little doubt that there has been a growth in what are described as 'professional and technical' groups within the workforce, where such workers are taken to represent the dominant tendency in what has come to be described as 'post industrial society', it is important to recognise the sociological sleight of hand involved. The majority of these new professionals, as well as their employers, have much to gain by concealing the real nature of the work, which often involves neither real skills nor the application of real knowledge (Kumar, 1978).

In sharp contrast to the 'proletarianisation of the professional' approach, other commentators, though agreeing that the professions have grown in size within the occupational system, argue that knowledge-based occupational groups will have increasing authority in 'post-industrial society'. The challenge of the principle of 'professionalism' to managerial authority will be successful because of the increasing significance of knowledge in the production process which involves specialised functions which are resistant to other forms of authority. Professional socialisation is an important part of this form of occupational organisation not only because of the 'knowledge' that is passed on, but as a consequence of lengthy periods of training in which common interests and experiences are shared with others undergoing the same process. As Freidson (1973) puts it:

> higher vocational education does not merely insert 'knowledge' into peoples heads, but also builds expectations and commitments not easily overcome by managerial or policy rationalization. Organised specialised occupational identities get constructed. Knowledge gets institutionalised as expertise. The structure of meanings and commitments can over-ride organisational goals or commitments.

An attempt has been made to bring these apparently opposing tendencies and interpretations together by an emphasis on the essentially dualistic character of the nature and organisation of professional knowledge (Jamous and Peloille, 1970). Professional practice, like any other productive activity, is seen as involving both a systematic body of knowledge which is used to justify competence and which can be expressed in the form of a set of rules (so called 'technicality') and aspects of knowledge which relate to the characteristics of professionals themselves and of the profession to which they belong. These include the uncertainties, mysteries and ideologies which create the conditions of uncertainty or 'indetermination', which in turn make monopolistic practice and resistance to external authority more likely. 'Technicality', on the other hand, exposes knowledge to codification and makes it vulnerable to external control; thus institutions of professional socialisation transmit such knowledge and provide legitimacy but at the same time expose knowledge to this form of codification. Professions are distinguished by a high 'indeterminacy/technicality ratio'. Indetermination is also important because it allows the holders of knowledge to share it only with those that they choose – the system is thus akin to that of the guilds. Professions are subject to a conflict between the two elements, the resolution of which will determine the character that a profession will take at a specific point in time.

But it is unclear from the previous argument what the condition for 'indetermination' might be, particularly the determinants of the differing degrees of power and privilege possessed by the professions, and this has led to a further attempt to resolve the problem of locating the professions in modern industrial society by reference to the capitalist mode of production (Johnson, 1976 and 1977). Here the professions are seen as involved in the various processes of capital, from the primary process of surplus value production to those of accounting, distribution and reproduction. Management professions and managerial techniques represent the primary function of control and surveillance of the productive process, while the accounting profession performs functions in the surveillance and distribution of capital. The process by which the system as a whole is maintained and replaced (or 're-produced') relates particularly to health and welfare professions; here such professions are involved in the process of applying definitions of such conditions as sickness and health, normal and deviant behaviour or educational success or failure.

But the state is also crucially involved in processes such as production and re-production and, in relation to the professions, performs a third-party interventionist function whereby the authority of either the professional or client to determine matters such as the content and subject of practice is challenged. This so-called heteronomous form of control can be compared with autonomous control, whereby authority in a group has been established by the members of that group. There are considerable variations in the form of heteronomous mediation, varying from a stipulation as to

who is to receive the service, leaving the professional to
determine the nature of the service (as in the British
National Health Service) to a definition not only of who will
receive the service but also how needs are to be met and
defined – the teaching and social work professions are seen
as representing this end of the continuum.

State intervention, therefore, has the effect of creating
whole categories of clients and this makes certain professions highly dependent on the social policies of the state.
The state has assumed the role of a patron to the occupational professions, a role which was previously performed
for the status profession by the highest social elite.   One
effect of this is that the definitions applied by the professions which relate to the re-production of the labour force
(in areas such as health, education and deviance) are also
matters of concern to the state and that such definitions can
be crucially influenced by the state.   The definitions of both
profession and the state may be congruent and the profession
may represent such 'official' definitions.   However, this
varies with the strength and stage of development of a profession.   In cases where the authority of the profession has
been relatively long established (as for example in medicine)
such definitions will be to a greater extent the property of
the profession; in cases where such authority is not so
established, definitions generated by agencies outside the
profession will become more powerful, as in the case of
social work where the crucial definitions (for example of
criminality or maladjustment) are made outside the professions.

Although the relationship between the state and the professions is very complex, in general professions will be
differentially rewarded in terms of their closeness to the
realisation of the direct function of capital; for example
medicine will be rewarded with greater privileges and power
than other professions and will as a result be able to claim
a greater degree of autonomy.

There is an important implication in this approach for the
status of the knowledge claimed by the profession, on which
is also based their claims to autonomy.   Rather than being
determined by its 'functional' significance for society in
general (Johnson, 1976)

> the very complexity of knowledge, the extent to which it
> remains 'esoteric', is determined by the degree to which
> it functions to promote and maintain capital ... the ideo-
> logy of professionalism will be an effective strategy only

when its claims coincide with and draw upon the dominant
ideological processes of capital.
Clearly this argument will apply also to the process of professional education and the educational institutions involved.

Despite the Marxist interpretation of the professions
having gained considerable support it is important to stress
the difficulty of accepting in any simple way a picture of the
professions as performing services for, and receiving
rewards from, the capitalist state. Certain features of the
professions, such as their power and dominance over the
occupational sphere and the autonomy of the individual professional in certain practice situations, point to the difficulties in maintaining this form of external control. For
example, Parry (1973) points to the occupational pre-
eminence achieved by the medical profession in which state
sponsorship was only one element. Again, the power of the
state to define client needs can also be exaggerated; 'the
State is not usually concerned with the ways in which the
client would define his needs but rather accepts the definition of the needs of the client as articulated by the profession' (ibid.).

The debate outlined above about the place of the professions in industrial society is sure to continue; what is
important to stress, whatever position is taken, is that the
links between the professions, their various internal processes and the wider society are often neglected by members
of the professions themselves in their own analysis of their
social situation. Indeed it is argued that where professional culture is under debate 'professional eyes do not see
the distortions in the world which this particular kind of
vision produces ... the modes of thought and action which
characterise any particular professional activity are not
observable from within professional culture' (Pearson,
1975).

Chapter three

The sociological study of professional education

(1) INTRODUCTION

Because the professions appear to be relatively autonomous, play important social functions and obtain high rewards, the common belief is that this requires a period of intense training and education (or in sociological terms 'socialisation') in which both practical skills and relevant forms of behaviour are learned. Thus, professional socialisation appears a relatively intense experience compared with other periods of socialisation (for example in school or family), and provides the sociologist with an opportunity, within a limited and defined context, to study processes such as personal change and social control. Another broader concern is with the relationship between professionalism and professional education. Forms of education and training have played an important role in the rise of the professions and in their prestigious position in modern societies. At the same time, some of the most strenuous criticisms of professionalism and the direction in which certain professions have developed has come from the training institutions and their staff and students.

These differing concerns have led to a number of different approaches to professional socialisation by sociologists which are briefly discussed in this chapter, including the model of professional socialisation which has been used as an organising framework for the book as a whole.

(2) ALTERNATIVE APPROACHES TO PROFESSIONAL SOCIALISATION

In attempting to approach the many issues involved in professional training, some sociologists have concentrated on
the link between present situations and behaviour within the
training process and the prediction of the future behaviour
of individuals in different situations. This emphasis reflects the conception held by many professionals of training
as 'future oriented' and for the sociologist opens up the difficult issue of relating 'present' and 'future' (Elliott, 1972).
For example, the Columbia studies of medical education
attempted to investigate such issues as the acquisition of
professional identity in medical school as a way of coping
with the future uncertainties of medical practice (Merton et
al., 1957), while the discontinuities between training and
later practice (or 'reality shock' as it is termed) have been
investigated in studies of teachers and army cadets (Lacey,
1977; Janovitz, 1960). However, other approaches have
concentrated on actions, interactions and activities in the
immediate present, particularly on the role of the student
and on student culture. Here the individual student is
oriented to short-term goals and the role that is being made
available to him is that of 'student' rather than 'practitioner'.
This approach is represented by the Kansas study of medical
education by Becker and his associates (Becker et al.,
1961): they comment that 'they /medical students/ do not act
as young doctors act, but rather as students act.'
  The two alternative approaches also imply very different
images of the way in which individuals learn their roles, and
reflect a very basic distinction between different theoretical
approaches in sociology.
  Until recently, much of the research in professional
socialisation was based upon the former set of ideas, of
which the Columbia medical education study is the leading
example. If any 'model' of the professional socialisation
process is suggested by such approaches, it is that of a
direct and largely unmediated transmission of values, attitudes and skills from knowledgeable and expert professionals
to aspirants who are seen in the role of neutral 'empty
vessels' and who come, over a period of time, to learn a
professional role which includes appropriate values, attitudes and skills (Merton et al., 1957). It is also important
to note the more general model of a profession on which this
is based. This is a mainly functionalist model in which a

profession is seen as a relatively homogeneous 'community' where members share identity, values, definitions of role and interests (Goode, 1957).

Although there is room in this model for variation, differentiation and even conflict, the basis is a common core to which newcomers are socialised. Because of the high prestige and power of the professions, and the opportunity for exploitation of the wider society this gives, socialisation and social control are of particular importance in order to insure the fulfilment of role obligations. A profession must therefore (ibid.)

> put its recruits through a set of adult socialisation processes and maintain procedures for continuing social controls over the practising professional ... professions almost isolate their recruits from important lay contacts for several years, furnish new ego ideals and reference groups, impress upon the recruit his absolute social dependence upon the profession for his further advancement and punish him for inappropriate attitudes or behaviour.

An implication of this approach is that one of the aims of the socialisation process is to turn out 'products' who are similar to, or may in the future become similar to, the socialisers in their playing of the professional role, and that this should make up an important criterion for judging the 'success' of socialisation. Basic to this view is also the idea that the skills, attitudes and values that individuals possess can be measured on a before/after basis to ascertain what has occurred during the socialisation process.

By contrast, the alternative approach stresses not only the importance of student culture and the strategies resulting from this as a response to problems the individual is encountering in the present, but also the complexity and multi-dimensional nature of professional socialisation. A particular feature of this approach is the stress laid upon the diversity of groupings or interests within a profession. These have been described by Bucher and Strauss (1961) as 'segments', each with its own history, conceptions of the 'real work' of the occupation and related sets of beliefs, theories and interpretive schemes. These authors include the following description of segments in their study:

> there are many identities, many values, and many interests. These amount not merely to differentiation or simple variation. They tend to become patterned and shared; coalitions develop and flourish – and in opposi-

tion to some others. We shall call these groupings within a profession 'segments' ... we shall develop the idea of professions as loose amalgamations of segments pursuing different objectives in different manners and more or less delicately held together under a common name at a particular period in history.

Segments may also be seen as embodying 'social movements', a series of activities carried out by a body of persons pursuing a specific object in a collective and organised way (Wilkinson, 1971). Professions may be heavily influenced by such movements at particular times in their history, or be the medium of conflict between competing movements. British social work in the late nineteenth century was characterised by a strong commitment to the alleviation of social problems and conflicts, although this reformist emphasis was soon to give way to more individualistic and therapeutic concerns. But the tension between these two orientations and the segments which represent them has continued and, in rather changed form, appear as the primary dichotomy today.

While all professions are loose amalgams of different segments, the theory of segments developed mainly in the medical profession where such differences are seen in their most extreme form. Members of the medical profession may seem to the outsider to share common ends, such as the better health and care of the patient. But there are many values which are not shared and over which there is conflict, a conflict which often stems from a struggle for recognition and status. As a result, statements of the 'mission' of particular segments are made which gives emphasis to the identity and claims of a particular group. For example, when surgical specialities such as urology were struggling to attain a status independent of general surgery they formulated a statement of mission which asserted that particular anatomical areas required special treatment which could only be given by those with particular knowledge of this speciality (Bucher and Strauss, 1961).

Differences of approach also characterise the 'core', or most characteristic, professional act. Here one of the most important examples is that of psychiatry, which for some practitioners means psycho-therapy or face-to-face interaction with clients. For others, treatment is mainly of a physical kind where there is little face-to-face interaction, while others specialise in preventive measures in the wider community. Other segments may not have such well-defined

core activities and may develop a range of auxiliary functions. For these reasons, the idea of a profession as a
community of colleagues is also difficult to sustain; where
a well-developed mission and a set of core activities exist,
it is all the more likely that members of a segment will have
more in common with those in associated professions outside
the medical field than those in their own profession.

The relevance of competing segments or movements to the
socialisation process is clear; each segment will have
rather differing ideas of the purposes of professional education, of the kind of programme that is relevant to such purposes, the kinds of experiences to which students should be
exposed, and the system of assessment and selection.
Thus, what happens to students depends upon which segments have power over the training programme. At its most
dramatic the situation can be described as a contest for the
allegiance of students, where the successful capture of the
loyalty of students is the prize. From the students' point
of view, their position is one of considerable vulnerability,
for in most cases they are virtually strangers in the new
world of the profession and the commitments they make to one
or other segment will have important repercussions throughout their career; hence, as Bucher and Strauss (1961) put
it, 'during their professional training students pick their
way through a maze of conflicting models and make momentous commitments thereby.'

While such segmental affiliations are characteristic of
professions at any stage in their development, in professions which are experiencing changes, such as greater
public recognition leading to increases in status and a
greater degree of professionalisation, there may be a particular segmental conflicts. These may centre upon the
challenge to existing training schools and their teachers
from newly established schools and a new generation of
teachers with different conceptions of the profession and
different educational experiences. Yet the existing
teachers and what they represent may retain an authority
which is often difficult to dislodge; as Hughes (1958) has
remarked:

> the early teachers are enthusiastic leaders of a movement,
> or protagonists of some new technique (such as casework)
> who have little conventional academic training ... they or
> some leader among them institute a curriculum which is
> likely to persist for some time and to be thought so sacred
> that to propose to alter it drastically is considered
> heretical.

It must be stressed, however, that from the student's point of view the main task is to complete the course successfully, to 'make out' or 'get through' in the immediate situation confronting them by negotiating successive tests of their competence.   This means that, to an extent at least, students' allegiance to the ideas or theories of a dominant segment may be transitory and highly instrumental, a factor often forgotten by the teachers who are in conflict over students' allegiances.   As Dingwall (1977) states in his study of health visitor training:

> most of the students recognised that lecturers were saying different things but saw these as surface differences rather than expressions of any basic conflict ... they were quite happy to invoke whatever theory seemed to be relevant in a given situation without regard to its consistency with any other theory that might be invoked on any other occasion.

(3) THE SOCIAL THEORIES OF TEACHERS

An alternative way of analysing the influences that teachers bring to the educational and socialising process is through a discussion of the kinds of general social theories implicit in their teaching, irrespective of segmental affiliation (Dingwall, 1977).

The term 'social theory' can be used to describe the types of knowledge of their societies (or 'social structures') drawn upon by members of these societies in order to 'make sense' of their everyday world and their activities within it.   Such theories can vary from the 'common-sense' theories of the 'man in the street' variety to the 'professional' or 'official' theories which members of certain occupations also claim to possess.   The structure of such theories has been given much attention by phenomenologists (Schutz, 1964) and includes possible strategies for the recognition and solution of 'troubles' or 'problems' encountered in everyday life. This forms the pattern of action for 'competent members' of a society (or lesser collectivity) compared to the situation of a 'stranger' who faces the problems of learning how to act and how to interpret the actions of others.   Students on professional courses of training face the dilemma of being both 'strangers' to a particular culture (that of their chosen profession), yet as adults are also held to be 'competent members' of the wider society.

Teachers will present a variety of 'theories' to students during a course of training and students will have, or begin to develop, their own set of theories about the world in which they find themselves (the latter will be described in a later chapter). Among the views presented to health visiting students Dingwall distinguishes a medical model, a social science model and a health visitor's model. The doctors were 'absolutists', having a vision of society as a war of all against all in which order was only preserved by coercion and control. Medicine was seen as an important agent of control mainly of a preventive kind over the basic biological human drives. The social scientists, so called 'professional' theorists, varied from 'evangelists' who felt they were in possession of a correct version of reality, to 'latitudinarians' who were doubtful about the possibility of such a version of reality existing, or of their right to propound it. Among the 'evangelist' group, the psychologists believed that human behaviour could be studied in a scientific manner which provided information on which could be based reliable choices or alternative courses of action by some appeal to 'objective facts'. The sociologists in this group also thought that their subject could provide reliable scientific knowledge of the world, although it was not yet in a position actually to perform this role; society was seen in terms of contending theories, such as consensus and conflict theories, and the problem was to make a synthesis of these.

The 'latitudinarians' were much less certain of their position and emphasised the fluidity and uncertainty of psychological and sociological phenomena. In particular they did not attempt to persaude the students of a 'true' version of reality and stressed instead the acquisition of certain principles by which reality could be analysed, based upon interactionism and a voluntaristic model of behaviour.

The tutors and fieldwork teachers were described as 'official theorists', although it was the college tutors who were found to have a fairly well worked out set of theories about their occupation, while fieldwork teachers drew more on 'common-sense' theorising. The tutors drew on medical and social science sources which, although acknowledged to be somewhat contradictory, were brought together to constitute their own approach to health visiting. Psychological and to a lesser extent sociological explanations were emphasised but biological or medical sources were largely discounted. The tutors offered an account of health visiting which was held to be 'rational' and in which intervention can

solve certain problems (for example of deviance from
accepted norms) yet recognising the limits to such solutions
set by social conditions and personality. Field teachers by
comparison stressed the importance of 'normal' categories of
behaviour and a consequently correctional view of deviance
which seeks to root it out and enforce certain standards.
In this they were close to 'common-sense' or 'lay' theorists
in such matters, and differed considerably from the less
judgmental and more 'open' stance adopted by the tutors.

(4) THE MULTI-DIMENSIONAL NATURE OF PROFESSIONAL SOCIALISATION

Turning to the social psychology of professional socialisation, an important issue is the degree to which the adult
personality can undergo change, and the character of these
changes.   The demands made upon the adult personality by
professional training can vary from little more than expansion of existing skills or an addition to knowledge to a complete discontinuity between earlier learning and the requirements of the present.   Brim (1968) suggests that in spite of
the new demands of marriage, family, work and mobility that
the individual has to cope with in early adult life, a durabil-
ity or continuity of personality is the more frequent experience, and that the degree of change can often be exaggerated.
   Thus, during the years of 'becoming a professional' or of
resocialisation from layman to professional status, develop-
mental socialisation or the acquisition of a role in adult
society for the young adult, is also proceeding.   These two
processes do not necessarily go on harmoniously and the
lateral, or 'life' roles, may blend quite uncomfortably with
roles in professional education (Oleson and Whittaker,
1968).   These lateral roles have often been ignored in
studies of professional socialisation, possibly because the
traditional professions which have been studied, such as
law, medicine and the military, have recruited mainly males
in early adulthood for whom the lateral roles were seen as
unimportant by comparison with the professional or occupational roles.   In other professional or semi-professional
situations where female recruitment has been important and
where age of entry may vary, such as teaching and social
work, the importance of lateral roles is more obvious.
   Professional socialisation may therefore be described as
multi-dimensional in character in that it accompanies other

forms of socialisation and is not exclusive of other role
relationships. Within the professional socialisation process, apart from role relationships with teachers, students
will also have relationships with patients, clients or pupils,
from whom they may acquire ideas, attitudes and ways of
behaving attributed to the profession by such 'non-official'
actors. These multiple agents of socialisation may also
function by viewing the student and acting towards him in
ways other than those in which the student would like to
view himself, or in which teachers would have the student
view himself (Oleson and Whittaker, 1968).

Professional socialisation is also multi-dimensional in the
sense that during this process the student may also experience a shift in his inner world, and acquires a new view of
the 'self', at the same time as the outer world is changing
through changing role performance. While these phenomenological aspects of the socialisation process are in theory
at work in all situations of professional education, in some
professions (particularly psycho-analysis and social work)
the growth of 'awareness of self' is seen as fundamental to
the whole learning process and to carrying out the professional role (Bucher, 1965; Bucher and Stelling, 1977).
Again, although the student is officially subordinate to the
teacher in professional education, and has no overt control
of the processes by which he is selected and over the actual
socialising programme through which he passes, this does
not mean that he has no power to shape his own role and take
an active part in his own education. Thus the student
assesses the demands of teachers, develops strategies in
relation to these demands and behaves in ways which are
felt to be compatible with what teachers require (Becker et
al., 1961). This active, or 'existential', view of the
student's career is in sharp contrast to the previous view of
the student as a passive 'recipient' of teaching. In an era
of student participation and student power, even the more
formal processes of the professional school, such as selection of students and even teachers, the teaching programme
and methods of teaching, may be much more open to student
control than ever before. For example, in some social
work courses in which students are mature and have practical experience, they have an active role in the planning and
running of courses (Payne and Dawson, 1979).

The general view suggested by theorists stressing an
interactionist or a multi-dimensional viewpoint is that the
student's progress through the socialising institution should

be regarded as raising a number of complex issues.
Students differ on entry and start from different positions.
Students differ in the extent to which they assimilate core
values, and display different rates and levels of progress.
This is related to the multiple agents of socialisation with
which the student is in contact. Finally, the student may
drop out, or deviate in some major way, from the career
path in the socialising institution, a situation which perhaps
throws more light than anything else on the central processes
of that institution.

The extreme of this approach is a plea for the abandoning
of the idea of 'socialisation' in the study of occupational
training (Dingwall, 1977). The term 'socialisation' is seen
as implying 'enculturation', or the passive internalisation of
a given social order abstracted from any other context.
In contrast, socialisation is rather seen as 'acculturation',
in which a group of newcomers tries to make sense of the
environment by attempting to acquire the knowledge that
would produce the kind of conduct which allows members of
the occupation to recognise such newcomers as 'competent'
members. This perspective, drawing as it does on concepts in ethno-methodology and interpretive sociology, has
much in common with previous approaches such as those of
Becker et al. (1961) and Davis (1968). It suggests that
students have an active role in interpreting the situation
through which they are passing, but also includes the idea of
the recognition and certification of competence through
selection and assessment processes by a group of established members of the occupational group whose definitions
are also crucial.

The functionalist and the interpretive/interactionist
approaches also imply different methods of research. The
idea of measuring and assessing the effects of professional
training implies a structured research design based upon a
sample of students interviewed at different points in time.
This was the basis of the Columbia studies (Merton et al.,
1957), although less structured material (including observation) was used, implying a sensitivity to social interactions
and culture. Becker's Kansas study emphasised participant observation, in which sociologists were attracted
to a class of medical students during a four-year period in
graduate school. This was also supplemented by material
from structured interviews at particular points in time.
Thus, instead of 'structures' and 'processes' being investigated on a 'taken for granted' level, there was an attempt

to understand these structures from the point of view of the
actors involved, and as resulting from their patterns of
interaction.

The importance of the theories of action and interaction
in the study of professional socialisation has been put in
this way by Becker et al. (1961):

> We studied what was of interest to the people we were
> investigating because we felt that in this way we would
> uncover the basic dimensions of the [medical] school as
> a social organisation and of the students' progress
> through it as a social psychological phenomenon. We
> made the assumption that, on analysis, the major con-
> cerns of the people we studied would reveal such basic
> dimensions and that we could learn most by concentrating
> on these concerns.... This meant that we began our
> study by looking for and inquiring about what concerned
> medical students and faculty and following up the connec-
> tions of these matters with each other and with still other
> phenomena.

Implicit in this idea is the attempt to portray 'how it looks'
to people passing through a particular system of organisation, rather than focusing on formal aspects of the organisation's structure and goals.

A particular concern in this type of approach is with
situations which seem to be matters of group tension or conflict (ibid.). If one of the objects of research is to uncover
the expectations surrounding the behaviour of social actors,
then one method may be the study of situations where these
expectations are violated or frustrated. It may be easier
to see 'how things work' when there is a situation of conflict than when things are going smoothly; in the latter
situation expectations may be taken for granted.

(5) STRUCTURAL AND SITUATIONAL VARIABLES

Some of the approaches to professional socialisation discussed so far have been formed into a model by Bucher and
Stelling (1977) which has been the starting-point for their
own research into socialisation in medicine, psychiatry and
biochemistry. An earlier version of this model (Bucher,
1965) also acted as a starting-point for the present author's
initial research on social work students. The first part of
this two-part model refers to certain structural variables,
including the nature of professions and the formal structure

of training institutions. The second set of variables, situational variables, are a function of the structural variables and refer to the social situations encountered by students which have the effect of socialisation.

Basic to the model is the idea of differing segmental affiliations in professions, as well as conflicts among segments. In considering structural variables such as the nature of the training programme, the kinds of experiences to which students should be exposed and the initial selection of students, it is important to know what influences are at work among the professional staff of the training institutions, which segments are represented and the form of relationships that exists to the wider professional community. Another important variable relates to the location of the department responsible for training; this may be part of a larger institution (such as a university), a situation which may influence a profession's ability to control its own training programme.

Situational variables, or the characteristics of situations in which trainees find themselves, will also vary. For example, training programmes will provide opportunities for trainees to perform the roles and do the work of the profession, as well as models on which the trainee can fashion his performances. But the reality of role playing may be diluted and the trainee may be merely 'playing at' doing such work; role models may be important indications of the work of a profession and close to the experiences of the trainees themselves, or seen as irrelevant to practice and remote from trainees. Other important characteristics include the student peer group (which will also be a function of the structure of the programme) and coaching, criticism and assessment, by which trainees know how they are progressing and eventually whether they have been successful in their training.

Finally, socialisation is likely to have an impact on trainees over time and it is important to set down the main stages and events which characterise this temporal experience. An important feature is the variation in levels of involvement and interest over the period of training courses, particularly the lowering of interest and morale at midpoints in training courses which is a familiar phenomenon both in the research literature and to professional educators.

Chapter four

Development of social work education

(1) EARLY DEVELOPMENTS

Social work, both as a profession and a social movement,
found its greatest sense of early purpose and identity in the
promotion of forms of training and education in the latter
part of the nineteenth century (Seed, 1973).   But the early
social workers were essentially amateurs.   The social
worker was a person of high status who attempted to help
the poor and unfortunate.   It was held that the necessary
preparation for this role was to be in touch with the philan-
thropic traditions of the middle class; for more practical
guidance the social worker was urged to reflect on his own
family life and his experiences of dealing with servants
(Timms, 1970).   Towards the end of the nineteenth century
the need for some form of training was being recognised
both by those in social work agencies and some of those
involved in university teaching.   One of the first initiatives
came from social workers associated with the Settlement
Movement, the latter designed to put university-trained
people in touch with the urban working classes.   By 1890
the Women's University Settlement in Southwark, together
with Octavia Hill who had already begun to train housing
workers, was organising courses of lectures for social
workers.   Such apprenticeship, agency-based type of
training gave way to specialised schools of social studies,
the first of which in Britain were established at the Universities of Liverpool (1904) and Birmingham (1907).   The first
school to be devoted entirely to social work training was in
Amsterdam in 1899; in America the first schools were set
up in Chicago (1903) and New York (1904).   Another initiative was the establishment of a training school by the leading

British social work organisation of the time, the Charity Organisation Society (COS), in which there was an attempt to combine practical training with social science studies. But the COS was also responsible for the stimulation of thinking about social work training in a wider context and recognised that outside support was needed. In fact, a number of the developments noted above had their origins in initiatives taken by the society (Mathews, 1978).

Yet there was considerable conflict over the issues raised by the development of training, some of which still have their echoes today. Some social work practitioners believed that the universities could not provide the practical training that was required and there were those in the universities who felt that this form of training was not one of the proper roles of the universities, or something over which they could have any control. But there were enough social workers and academics who supported the involvement of the universities in this area to lay the foundations of what became known as the 'social training movement' and to assist in the development of university departments in which social work training was given (Jones, 1964). In spite of the decline in the involvement of some social scientists because of their desire to find a more respectable and 'scientific' basis for their operations, the movement prospered. But at first the social studies departments were to be a poor relation within the universities by comparison with more established departments, their lowly status emphasised by being accommodated often in converted houses on remote corners of the campus or distant parts of the city.

From the standpoint of contemporary social work education, such beginnings are often (possibly nostalgically) seen as being in advance of their time. One reason was because of the realistic attempt to relate theory to practice and to test out principles through practice and a knowledge of social conditions (Mathews, 1978). Here the availability of sociology and the enthusiasm of some of the early sociologists was important, and sociology and social work were often linked in the same university department. The Third International Survey of Social Work Education (United Nations, 1958) notes that 'the pioneers in these "under-developed" areas of Amsterdam, Chicago, London and New York discovered empirically what would be regarded at the present day as essentially the right answers about the subjects and methods of social work education.'

The evolution of social work education illustrates the

importance, particularly for the newly emerging occupational professions with little or no histories of elite status,
of intervention and recognition by elements outside the occupation itself.   In the early period it was clear that the
development of social work education was encouraged by
those who were influential in access to and the development
of relevant knowledge – the university teachers.

The experiences of the First World War intensified demand
for social workers and increased the number of universities
involved in the training process, and there was the obvious
need to form some kind of organisation to discuss issues
related to training.   Consequently the Joint University
Council for Social Studies (today the Joint University Council for Social and Public Administration) was formed to co-
ordinate the work of the social studies departments.   While
the majority of workers were still untrained, the University
Certificate or Diploma in Social Studies was to be the basic
qualification in social work until after the Second World War.
However, no specialised schools of social work training
emerged at this time in Britain along the lines of the American university schools of social work; again a comparison
could also be drawn between the universities' involvement in
setting up specialised training schools for the medical and
teaching profession, and their lack of a similar initiative in
the case of social work.

The major exception to this pattern of training were
courses training workers for specific areas of work, such
as the Certificate of the Institute of Almoners or the Mental
Health course at the London School of Economics, the latter
established in 1927.   Some students went on from basic
social studies courses to such forms of specialised training,
the latter incorporating new forms of psychological knowledge combined with a social casework approach.   The
significance of these specialised courses and the occupational associations with which they were associated (the
Institute of Almoners and the Association of Psychiatric
Social Workers) was that only those with the appropriate
qualifications were admitted to full membership, although
there was no way in which the appointment of non-members
to social work posts could be prevented.   However, the
work of these associations represents the first attempt at
some form of control of entry to these occupations, and thus
an important step towards occupational professionalism in
social work.   Moreover, these associations and their
leaders formed an elite (consisting mainly of women) who

were to be influential in the development of social work
training and practice in the following decades. Out of 60
students who received the Mental Health Certificate between
1931 and 1934, one-third became psychiatric social workers
in child guidance clinics, the remainder working in general
or mental hospitals and a variety of other settings both
statutory and voluntary. The majority were also women,
although there were still more male probation officers than
female probation officers, almoners and psychiatric social
workers put together (Walton, 1975).

(2) A CHANGE OF DIRECTION

The Second World War, and its aftermath, created an entirely new situation for social work training. The war had
shown how useful social workers could be in times of stress
and change, for example in coping with the social and psychological effects of evacuation and the mobilisation of the
adult population for both active service and other forms of
war work (Titmus, 1950). The post-war social legislation,
particularly the institution of social insurance on a universal
basis and the dismantling of the Poor Law had drastically
altered the situation in which social workers operated, apart
from creating renewed demands for more trained workers.
The effects of such new developments were to challenge the
social training movement as an effective basis for the training of social workers (Jones, 1964). One development was
an increase in the number of degree courses in social studies
departments, including those in social administration. The
latter had grown as an academic subject under the stimulus
of the social legislation of the Welfare State, and as a result
of the work of Titmus and his colleagues at the London
School of Economics and academics elsewhere. This indicated a line of development for the social studies departments
that was an alternative to social work training, and which
represented a tradition which was increasingly in competition with it for resources, recognition and theoretical
legitimacy.
    There was also a concern on the part of the state to
develop social work and appropriate forms of training,
although this centred on the welfare of specific groups
rather than support for the comprehensive development of
social work. An example is that of the establishment of
specialised services for children, following the report of

the Curtis Committee in 1948.   This involved the establishment of new local government departments with central responsibility being taken by the Home Office, and with relevant
training courses of a university type.   The importance of
this development was that it gave an opportunity (under the
Children Act, 1948) for the establishment of a social work
specialism that was, unlike some other areas of social work,
independent of the medical profession and which gave rise to
administrative positions of seniority and importance within
the new structure (Walton, 1975).   It should also be added
that this development was supported by advances in psychology and sociology which were highly relevant to issues and
policies surrounding the family and its relationship to the
wider society.   As a result of the 1948 Act seven courses
for child-care workers were established and students were
grant aided from central government funds.   In addition,
the majority of students in probation, almoning and psychiatric social work were similarly grant aided, and the Home
Office and the Ministry of Health took an active part in
training (Jones, 1964).

In spite of such developments, the total number of students
entering full professional training courses was still small,
only 98 in the year 1950-1 (ibid.; see Table 4.1), most
universities relying at that time on non-graduate, pre-pro-
fessional certificate courses.   It is arguable that there was
a failure to establish social work training on an adequate
and coherent basis during this early post-war period in
which many innovations in welfare were emerging – it is also
argued that this inadequacy, particularly in the face of
rising demands for social workers, characterised the entire
period up to the 1970s (Walton, 1975).   By the year 1962-3
the number entering professional courses had risen to 302,
an increase of 208 per cent and representing a doubling of
the percentage that these students made up of all social
studies students compared to 1950-1.   Certificate course
students had declined by 42 per cent over the period, but
degree course students had increased by 210 per cent.   The
number of departments providing professional social work
training courses had increased to 17, but development was
uneven, the London School of Economics and Liverpool University accounting for over a half of all such students.   The
inadequate numbers of students, seen against the rising
demand for social workers, was due partly to a lack of grant
aid other than to specialised areas such as child care and
probation, and the courses were still filled by predominantly

TABLE 4.1 Students entering social studies departments in 1950, 1955, 1960 and 1962 (source: Jones, 1964)

	Degree	Non-graduate certificate	Postgraduate diploma	Professional courses	Total
1950–1	146	387	185	98	824
1955–6	216	306	111	147	799
1960–1	322	255	192	233	1029
1962–3	453	223	207	302	1219
% increase/ decrease 1950–62	+210.3	–42.4	+11.9	+208.2	+47.9

female and middle-class students.   The proportion of males
completing social studies courses in the period 1950-60 was
under one-third.

A background to this slow development was the equivocal
nature of the involvement of the state.   The architects of
the Welfare State saw little place for social work within it,
placing their faith in social reform involving state intervention in the realm of economic and social inequality.   This
was a far cry from the social work tradition of the late nineteenth and early twentieth centuries in which the relief of
poverty was accompanied by moral exhortation.   Beveridge
was opposed to such a policy on the grounds that while it
would encourage contact between different social classes it
ignored the basically economic causes   of poverty (Harris,
1977; cited in Parry and Parry, 1979) and 'nowhere ...
among the official conceptions of the welfare state was a
place conceived for social work' (Parry and Parry, 1979).
In fact, the situation was part of a long-running conflict
between the vision of social work promoted largely by the
COS and that of a reformed and reconstructed society based
upon the beliefs of their liberal and socialist critics.

But there were a number of considerations that led to a
convergence between social work and the state, resulting
from the unintended rather than the intended consequences of
state intervention.   The modern Welfare State involved the
break up of the old Poor Law and therefore meant the
establishment of new services for such groups as the aged
and the mentally ill.   The emergence in post-1945 Britain
of the principle of social insurance for all meant that social
workers could separate the relief of poverty from the provision of non-material services.

This provided an opportunity for social workers to establish themselves independently of the provision of economic
relief and thus enabled them to offer their services to the
population in general on an entirely different basis.   The
need for trained workers for such services was self-evident,
and is well illustrated by the rise of the children's service,
in which social workers could offer their services to children and their families on the basis of specialised knowledge
and professional training, albeit within the limitations of
local government service.   As Parry and Parry (1979)
comment

the new child care service was quickly judged to have gone
further than Probation in respect of both standards of
recruitment and training, and in the level of responsibili-

ties given to social workers.   It brought social workers
with professional aspirations into the local authorities
alongside already established departments employing professionals, such as education ... the Childrens Act
therefore was an important landmark in the formation of a
partnership between social work and the State.

Another important development was the establishment of a
non-specialist generic course of training at the London
School of Economics, in 1954.   With American developments
in mind, Younghusband had advocated in her 1947 report on
the condition of British social work the foundation of a
School of Social Work as a graduate school within a university in which research as well as teaching would be the aim.
After much discussion of the idea a scheme for post-graduate education aimed to produce good general practitioners
in social work was accepted and the course started at the
London School of Economics in 1954.   While the scheme was
much more modest than the original proposal, the course was
important because it provided a model for generic training
and for the integration of social work around a common professional base, as opposed to the fragmented specialised
training which was developing.   It was to be an important
straw in the wind as far as the future of social work training
was concerned and was to provide the basis of a struggle for
dominance with the specialist branches of the profession in
later years (this is fully described in chapter 5).   But the
real problem facing social work was that of a lack of trained
workers, with little hope of rapid expansion through the
traditional means of the universities.

(3) THE YOUNGHUSBAND REPORT 1959

By far the most important response to the situation was the
Younghusband Report (1959) into the training of workers in
the local authority health and welfare services.   In 1956,
93 per cent of local authority staff in this area were untrained, and a further demand for training was implicit in
the community care proposals of the Mental Health Act,
1959.   The Younghusband Report proposed to train workers
for such services outside the universities, and for them to
occupy the middle strand in a three-tier system, the lowest
tier to be that of welfare assistant and the upper to be that
of university trained workers who would administer the service.   The latter would be responsible for intensive work

on more difficult problems and would have a teaching function in respect of workers with less training. The second
tier of workers would have a two-year training combining
theory and practice, and welfare assistants would be given
in-service training.

The Report was also important because it created a
national body for the administration and planning of social
work education, the Council for Training in Social Work
(CTSW) and a staff college for the training of teachers and
senior administrators (the National Institute for Social
Work), which embodied some of the principles of the school
of social work that had been thwarted in the 1950s. The
CTSW assumed responsibility for promotion and recognition
of courses, for setting standards and for the award of a
National Certificate in Social Work for the newly founded
courses. It worked alongside two other training councils
(in child care and probation), and courses also ran under the
auspices of professional associations, the Institute of
Medical Social Workers and the Association of Psychiatric
Social Workers.

The new educational system was rapidly constructed; the
educational institutions involved (such as colleges of further
education) welcomed the courses as they increased their
amount of advanced level work. By 1967, 217 certificates
had been awarded for those completing the basic two-year
courses (Walton, 1975). Such courses were also important
in providing an avenue for male recruits (as also did the
child-care courses - by 1976 nearly two-fifths of field officers were men), and for training those already in post on
the basis of secondment. The courses embodied a generic
principle and were an important impetus to the spread of
this idea, and therefore an impetus towards greater professionalism and unity. The generic principle was also
spreading within the universities; as the separate professional bodies began to accept generic training as the basis
for membership, more universities mounted such courses,
which by the 1960s were to include four-year degree
courses in applied social studies with a professional qualification in social work. By the 1970s this type of course was
to become a basic part of the work of social studies departments in universities and polytechnics.

(4) THE SEEBOHM REPORT AND ITS AFTERMATH

However, during the 1960s confusion was still caused by
the number of different courses of training and administering
councils, as well as settings for different forms of social
work. Legislation following the Seebohm Committee Report
(1968) created unified social work departments in local
authorities in which existing specialisms were amalgamated.
A similar unification of social work training was also proposed, and a new training council to replace the existing
councils was set up in 1971. This, the Central Council
for the Education and Training of Social Workers (CCETSW),
assumed responsibility for the training of most social
workers and awarded the Certificate of Qualification in
Social Work (CQSW) to those students who had successfully
completed a course validated by the Council. The Council
took responsibility for the development and oversight of a
social work training programme for the whole country.

The Seebohm Report also stressed the importance of
establishing proper patterns of recruitment, training and a
career structure and rewards comparable to other areas of
local government administration, such as teaching. While
some movement towards this has been made, it is important
to stress that this has involved a negotiated agreement
between social workers(and their aspirations for professional status), and the new organisational and managerial
approach in central and local government. The mixture
might be called 'bureau-professionalism' (Parry and Parry,
1979), as opposed to the autonomous professionalism
favoured by some leading social workers, in which control
is vested in the hands of professionals. Instead, the
current structure allows a measure of professional control
which could increase through the reduction in the number of
the untrained occupying social work posts. While nearly
3,500 students were emerging from all courses of professional training leading to the CQSW by 1979 (CCETSW,
1980a), it was estimated that less than two-fifths of local
authority social workers had recognised professional
training.

Finally in 1970 a number of specialist professional associations representing most of the different areas of social
work practice, each with its own history and identity, came
together to form one professional association, the British
Association of Social Workers. Paradoxically, the merging of existing specialist associations, which formerly

had certain responsibilities for training and with established registers of members, into an umbrella association
with no direct training function might be seen as something
of a setback for professionalisation in social work (Parry
and Parry, 1979). Although the CCETSW had members of
the social work profession both as council members and
professional advisors, the control of social work training
had become diversified among a number of interests, including the state represented by the Department of Health and
Social Security (which finances the Council) as well as
academic and other representation.

(5) SOCIAL WORK EDUCATION OUTSIDE THE UNIVERSITIES

The controversy which surrounded, and still surrounds,
the introduction of courses of training in social work outside the universities stems largely from the challenge they
represent to the idea of a profession which bases its claims
to professional status partly on a university-trained and
mainly graduate body of workers. Such courses were
introduced in 1960, yet the question of whether the innovation of full, professional training outside the universities
has threatened the standard of students and courses is still
debated (Stevenson, 1976). The controversy can be
approached by reference to the immediate reactions to the
Younghusband Report of 1959.
Most commentators recognised the need to develop a
trained corps of workers in an important area of the social
services hitherto almost untouched by social work methods
and theories. On the other hand, the training of non-
graduates, or those without some kind of university qualification, in institutions outside the universities, and thus the
differentiation of a hitherto trained elite of workers was
also seen as constituting a threat to the professional claims
of social work and to the recognition of that status by other
professions. Thus doubts were expressed both about the
capacities of the educational institutions chosen for the new
training, and the capacities of the trainees themselves.
The colleges of further education were thought to be inadequate because of a specialisation in 'dull, examination
based "passing of notes" teaching' (Willcocks, 1959). An
alternative locale for the new courses was seen by some
critics as the university extra mural departments where

standards were of an appropriate kind and which would be suitable to a new venture such as the proposed courses. Another problem was raised by the admission to training of students with no previous experience of higher education, and the question arose of 'how to teach ideas, hypotheses and the uncertainties of human behaviour to groups of people who may find abstraction difficult and who will press for certainty and "facts"' (Wright, 1961). Without the scepticism which is supposed to come from university education, such students would, it was felt, treat the theories and ideas encountered on social work courses as revealed truth and so create the danger that existing prejudices would become justified by jargon and science.

In wrestling with these problems social workers were forced to consider again an old dilemma – the pursuit of full professional status, implying a body of workers with uniform and probably graduate training, together with the 'esprit de corps' of the recognised professions, at the price of a broader 'mission' in which different levels of training are distinguished and a wider body of workers receive some form of training. Thus to extend general training outside the universities, with all the doubts about standards that this implied, 'may sound the death knell of the profession' (Waldron, 1959). Another question surrounded the content and status of the university courses – could these in fact be distinguished from other forms of social work training? In attempting to answer such questions, most commentators appeared to accept the inevitability of the 'new order', even at the price of professional martyrdom. Thus Waldron stated:

> we have no alternative but a future in which a larger
> group of social workers become well trained, outside the
> universities, to discern more clearly the way in which
> they help clients with their difficulties in social function-
> ing ... and it could be that the client is the better served
> by this arrangement, although a gestating profession has
> aborted.

Clearly the distinction between two types of trained worker, the 'trained' and the 'professionally trained' made by the Younghusband Committee was an ingenious device to solve this dilemma; in this sense 'full' professional status was reserved for the university–trained worker. But this distinction appears now to be quite impracticable, for it seems almost impossible to justify or construct a training programme for social workers outside universities without

inculcating many of the attitudes and values which were
general in the profession (McDougall, 1962). It has also
been difficult for employers to make a distinction of this
kind.

This distinction has also been criticised in another way.
Wootton (1959) suggests that the model adopted for the proposed tripartite structure of training and practice was a
medical one; thus nurses do much routine work under the
supervision of doctors and general practitioners call in the
help of consultants in specially difficult cases. The middle-
tier, non-university trained social worker would be forced
to adopt the same role. The difficulty about the analogy lies
in the fundamental differences between the professions.
Whereas the medical profession has accumulated a great deal
of specialised knowledge, the same cannot be said for social
work even when recent advances in social science knowledge
are taken into account. Thus 'skills' in social work are
difficult to define and even more difficult is the task of
dividing up cases into different types to which different
levels of skills can be applied. The suggested structure is
attributed by Wootton to 'the contemporary craze for professionalism' to which the Report gives, in her opinion,
unqualified and undiscriminating blessing. Here the 'skills'
required of social workers are knowledge of the social services rather than the handling of the 'relationship' with the
client.

More recently a further extension of training in the non-
university sector has been made in the form of courses for
workers whose responsibilities do not require full social
work training (CCETSW, 1975). The Certificate in Social
Service course has a variety of objectives, including the
provision of more specialised training for those who have
already trained in the generic system. In this sense one
of the consequences of such courses may be to lessen the
differences between social workers working at different
levels of skill, and who have been trained within different
educational traditions.

(6) CONCLUSION

The recent history of social work education has been one of
slow movement towards a form of occupational professionalism in which the specialisms formed as a result of ad hoc
developments of policy have been forged into some kind of

unity: the post-war period has seen 'the barriers between
fields of practice slowly and painfully dismantled in the
interests of creating a unified profession' (Stevenson,
1976).   Such changes have reflected pressure in the world
outside social work as well as the drive towards professionalism from within.   Yet these changes have produced or
exacerbated other problems.   One is that the specialisa-
tions characteristic of the earlier days of training have
been too easily set aside in the drive to produce more
trained workers through the generic method.   This has
resulted in some scepticism about the knowledge and skills
of contemporary social workers in facing some of the more
intransigent problems - for example those relating to particular social groups, or work in depth with families with
multiple problems.   This scepticism is reflected in comments by both social workers and external critics, and some
of the latter (Brewer and Lait, 1980) reiterate the earlier
comments of Wootton that much of the knowledge that is
passed on in training rests upon untested theories.   Consequently the differences between the work of the trained and
the untrained are hard to substantiate.

Another movement from within social work has been the
growing criticism of both social work education and of conditions of employment and financial rewards from social
workers who are critical of the drive for unity and increased
professionalism.   This has taken the form of organised
trade unionism and of action by radical groups or segments
within the profession.   These have argued for a different
set of alliances than those prescribed by traditional professionalism, and for social work education to reflect a concern for what is held to be the real needs of clients and their
communities (Heraud, 1973).

These differing currents of opinion make for a confused
and changing situation and there seems every reason to
believe that social work education, as well as the organisation of practice, will not retain their present form and function in the face of the controversies that are at present
surrounding them.

Chapter five

Professional communities and theories

(1) INTRODUCTION

The development of any profession is clearly based upon
factors, particularly that of a recognisable and specialised
knowledge base, which serves to unify a group of hitherto
more or less disparate individuals or groups into an effective entity which can claim a monopoly over a service.
This is made easier by the codification and formalisation of
knowledge which means that it can be more readily passed
on to new members of the profession.

But while professions may have achieved a form of unity
at a particular point in time, it is also clear that there is a
tendency to movement and change, in relation both to the
development of new knowledge and to social and political
currents in the wider society. The trend towards unity is
therefore threatened from time to time by widely differing
tendencies within a profession represented by rival groupings each with its own conceptions of the real nature of the
profession. These have been described in chapter 3 as
'segments', and it was suggested that segmental affiliations
will have a crucial significance for the socialisation process. In this chapter the nature of segmental affiliations
in social work will be discussed first in terms of distinctions that have been made between the 'therapeutic',
'reformist' and 'radical' segments, and second in terms of
the conflict between 'generic' and 'specialist' principles.

One of the most characteristic ways in which differing
segments have been expressed in social work is in terms of
'social reform' and 'therapy'. Meyer (1967) describes
these orientations in the following way:

In its history social work has long had a double focus: on

social reform on the one hand; and on facilitating adjustment of individuals to existing situations, on the other.
These two themes reappear in various forms: as environ-
mental manipulation or promotion of psychological functioning; as concern with people through mass programs;
or as casework with persons 'one by one'. Social
workers have been conscious of these two approaches to
social welfare and have often sought to reconcile them.
Mary Richmond, symbol of the case by case approach, is
reported to have said to Florence Kelly, symbol of reform
in the grand style; 'We work on the same programme. I
work on the retail end of it, but you work on the whole-
sale'. But these two viewpoints are still not integrated,
and both are represented by acknowledged spokesmen for
the profession.

In their various ways such segments are fairly clearly
represented in social work education, although it is probably true to say that in Britain the distinctions have not
(until very recently) been as clear cut as elsewhere and that
there are a variety of forms of accommodation between different and potentially conflicting groups. Such distinctions
also have considerable implication for professionalism, and
it has been argued that social reform is a less certain basis
for the successful assertion of claims for professional
status than a therapeutic standpoint, particularly because
the latter implies some common ground with the established
professional practices and techniques of medicine (Heraud,
1970).

Since the 1960s, the social and political context in which
social work in Britain is practised has changed dramatically.
This is partly a reflection of organisational changes in social
work, particularly the creation of unified local authority
departments which resulted from the Seebohm Report of
1968 and the development of the British Association of
Social Workers (BASW) out of a number of separate associations. The implications of such changes are difficult to
interpret; they have been seen as promoting professionalism
and increasing the professional status of social work, but it
is also argued that such developments promote a greater
diversity of work with a greater variety of potential clients
(Cypher, 1975). Many of these developments have attracted
criticism, both for the status seeking that seemed implicit
in professionalism and because of the large-scale and more
impersonal bureaucratic structures that were being created.
By the early 1970s there was evidence that the reformist

segment within social work was gaining strength (Lees,
1971; Cypher, 1975).

At the same time both therapists and reformists have been
subject to criticism from the radical left, who have attempted to place the recent developments in social work, particularly the twin growth of professionalism and bureaucracy,
within the context of industrial capitalism (Bailey and
Brake, 1975). While many radicals themselves would dis-
pute that an agreed programme for action yet existed, or
was even possible in view of the deeply embedded control
functions of social work, there is no doubt that a radical,
activist segment within social work has grown in the recent
past and is exemplified in the existence of particular groups
and policies, including social work teachers with a specifically Marxist orientation (see Corrigan and Leonard, 1978).
This programme includes not only radicalising activists
within the white-collar unions related to social work, but
also the formation of alliances with clients and involvement
'in agitational and ideological aspects of the class struggle
as it applies to their own field of work' (Wilson, 1977).
Such developments have done severe damage to the image of
social work as a unified profession; as Pearson (1975)
remarks 'we do our students a disservice when we cling to
the idea of social work as a unitary profession. Social
work is a highly segmented profession; there are many
legitimate positions which can be adopted within it.' These
sentiments also seem to be shared by a substantial number of
leading social work teachers; in a response to a recent
paper on social work education by a senior social work education administrator (CCETSW, 1977), the majority opposed
the idea that social work was (or should be) based upon a
shared and explicit set of values and that it was a mistake to
pursue this form of consensus (CCETSW, 1979).

The idea of segmental affiliations is but one way of charac-
terising the immense diversity of social work. An alternative point of departure is to identify other types of direc-
tional thrusts each with distinctive but sometimes overlapping
goals and which are linked with political trends in the wider
society. Pritchard and Taylor (1978) have identified the
competing frames of reference in social work as the moral-
ethical, the psycho-pathological, the psycho-social and the
radical political. This formulation points to the diversity
of interests found in the category which has so far been described as 'therapeutic' and also links together within the
radical perspective approaches which have so far been dis-

tinguished as 'reformist' and 'radical activist'. The interpretation in the remainder of this chapter will be that there
are considerable differences between the latter perspectives.

Whatever distinctions are maintained the point of agreement lies in viewing social work and the educational processes involved in essentially political and ideological
contexts.

(2) SEGMENTS IN PRACTICE

The academic and fieldwork teachers in the research
courses in the late 1960s exhibited a variety of segmental
affiliations. While a third of the teachers were qualified in
traditional social work specialities (psychiatric social
workers being the largest group, followed by medical social
work and probation), another third had qualified through
generic (or applied social studies) training, and several
more had two-year Certificates in Social Work or post-
graduate degree qualifications. Overall, the latter group
of teachers trained in the 'generic' tradition during the
1950s and 1960s were numerically in the ascendency.
Generic ideas were also clearly illustrated in the accounts
most of the tutors gave of their work, irrespective of therapeutic or reformist influences.

There was, however, a clear emphasis on a therapeutic
orientation among the majority of the college teachers,
illustrated by this extract from the account of one of the
technical college teachers:

At X College we consider casework to be the crucial task
because it has so much to do with practice. If one con-
siders other methods of social work we feel that skills
and knowledge for practice of casework are essential for
other methods (group and community work) ... we give
students idea that there is a method in social work –
study/diagnosis/treatment – most of them aren't aware of
it. Before you begin to teach them the methods you talk
about ethics and values involved in social work – the
principles underlying casework ... I was brought up on
Biestek and Hamilton and don't know whether things have
changed very much. We use the Hollis textbook as the
base now. I have tried to integrate some of the dynamic
theories of personality with as much sociological theory
as I know; basically we use a kind of eclectic Freudian

theory which is fairly common among caseworkers in this
country, but I don't want to give the impression we give
too much weight to this in teaching ... I tend to see
things and people in an individual way; each of the people
I'm teaching I see as individuals. In general I like to
see a person at the end of the course as unprejudiced as
possible about social issues, reasonably stable and
mature; enough aware of themselves and their own reactions so that they don't want to influence their clients to
be like them; somebody not so obsessed with the study of
individual people (which is so fascinating) that they don't
look at external issues like poverty; somebody who can
really help people find their own way through their difficulties instead of trying to find a way for them; somebody
not afraid to get involved in best possible way with
clients – not distant and cold but not too over involved.

In addition, this social work teacher also had a fairly
clear definition of the tutor's role which is seen in part as
an active concern for the impact of the course on the personality of the individual student. There is also a considerable link between the tutor/student and social worker/client
relationship, and between the kinds of theories used in practice and in dealings with students. In addition, relationships – both actual and desired – outside teaching are with
other social work practitioners and with specialised and
exclusive professional associations. Cypher (1975) describes therapists as 'viewing individual adjustment as the
object of their professional intervention and who believe that
services should be provided for all social groups in the
community.'

The outlines of an alternative professional identification
also appeared among a minority of teachers on the research
courses, although this 'reformist' orientation (Meyer, 1967;
Cypher, 1975) was expressed somewhat tentatively. Only
in one instance in the research courses was a reformist
identification dominant for an individual tutor:

I hope that students will get some idea of their role in
relation to its setting and to the pressures and values of
society, also that they will see their work in some kind of
historical perspective and understand change and the
reasons for change. My focus is not just on the Health
and Welfare services because one attempts to be generic
and talk about the organisation of all services; see the
student as a person working in any of them; interested in
how he works in an organisation and how that organisation

works within the framework of society ... my purpose is
not concerned with the casework element in social work
and I have reservations about the extent to which casework can be used in certain situations ... Donnison's
approach to organisations is very much what interests me,
particularly his theories of change in organisations and
how policy is shaped ... he draws attention to the fact
that change comes from people he calls the 'providers' in
the social services; providers are social workers but
also administrators; this has important implications
because it puts responsibility on the providers not just
vis à vis clients in the face to face relationship but vis à
vis policy and change in the whole service. This puts a
new emphasis on the [administrators'] role and also
brings social workers and administrators much closer
together. He refuses to draw a distinction, something
the students are not very keen on; this is what influences
all my teaching ... extremely unhappy in role as tutor and
have no idea of the function. Don't understand it and go
around asking what supposed to do. Everybody says they
feel the same but some can instinctively cope with the
situation ... there is nothing written down about the tutor
function but there is an assumption that one must beware
not to be a caseworker and hold onto role as teacher ...
I'm not sure whether tutorial relationship should become
therapeutic and wouldn't want to do it myself ... I'm very
uncomfortable about the social work tutoring thing.

By contrast to the previous illustration, there is a very
different theoretical focus (the influence of generic thinking
is much clearer than in the previous case) which involves
less clarity and certainty about the role and functions of the
social work tutor. In addition to this, actual and desired
relationships outside the teaching role are with administrators, researchers and political pressure groups rather than
practitioner and professional associations. Cypher (1975)
defines 'reformists' as favouring 'some change in the social
environment as the object of their work with clients, without
restricting the service only to the disadvantaged.'

These brief profiles suggest the outlines of differing segments within social work in the late 1960s, and which could
be expected to have an impact on the way students experience
a course of training and on the approach of teachers to their
tasks. In recent years the distinction between the beliefs
and theories illustrated by teachers on the research courses
have become more pronounced and Cypher (1975) has attemp-

ted to categorise the variety of segments in British social
work in the mid-1970s (see Table 5.1), based upon Epstein's
(1970) earlier work on the relationship between professionalism and political attitudes in American social work.   The
segments are distinguished by attitudes to both individual
adjustment and social reform and the provision of services
on a universal or selective basis.   To the existing categories of 'therapists' and 'reformists' have been added 'traditionalists' and 'activists'.   Traditionalists describes those
working for change or adjustment in the individual, yet pre-
ferring to concentrate services on the disadvantaged.
Activists form a category in which there is a concern with
remedying inequalities and for concentrating services on the
disadvantaged together with a concentrated drive to secure
social change.   But the activists were an ambiguous group,
for also included were those who were equally concerned
with remedying inequality but who believed that a concentra-
tion only on the disadvantaged was stigmatising.   But a clear
difference between activists and others emerged in attitudes
to BASW, where the former believed that the association
should involve itself in the promotion of individual and community welfare (as against more traditional professional
objectives) and who saw the association as a vehicle for the
expression and promotion of radical concerns and activities.
As Cypher comments 'clearly we have a group with a genuine
radical orientation properly described as activists.'
     While the therapists and reformists are represented in all
the sections of BASW, in the latter case this is most strongly
in evidence in the mental health field.   This latter section
and those working in child care also claimed all the activists
in this study (see Table 5.1).
     While the category that is loosely defined as radical or
activist is made up of a number of widely differing groups
and orientations, one of the most important in educational
terms has been that dominated by a specifically Marxist set
of beliefs and the attempt to develop a Marxist theory of
practice in social work.   Thus to the accounts of the therapist and reformist teachers given above can be added that of
social work teachers with a very different educational philosophy.   Here Corrigan and Leonard (1978) attempt to re-
assess the relationship between the individual, society and
social work:

     In social work, we must begin to understand individual
     experience and the features of individual personality as a
     reflection of the social relations of production and of the

TABLE 5.1 Goal orientation of respondents by sectional membership*
(source: Cypher, 1975)

	Therapists (%)	Traditionalists (%)	Reformists (%)	Activists (%)
Physical illness	40	0	30	0
Mental health	25	0	44	25
Child and family social work	39	7	18	25
Treatment of offenders	33	17	33	0
All sections	47	7	28	18

* Not all respondents were classifiable

contradictions within those relations. This means
understanding them not only in relation to the family as a
reflection, at least in part, of the dominant economic
structure but also in the other wider structures with which
individuals interact. In this way, the analysis that social
workers undertake of individual and social situations is
not then simply a dichotomy between understanding the
individual and understanding the social structure.
Rather, because individuals are seen as directly related
to their social circumstances, with their experience and
personality embedded in the structure, and the structure
embedded in them, we begin to see a clear connection
between individual and structural factors. For social
workers, this comes out most clearly, at quite a small
level, in the nature of the social relationships which exist
between welfare clients and those with whom they interact
most intimately.... In short, we must, as social
workers, come to understand how the contradictions
within the capitalist system are reflected in the contradictions within individuals and families.... The point is to
transform our understanding with the individual client in a
way that enables the relevance of the wider features of the
capitalist system to be understood and acted upon.

The growth of reformist and activist or radical segments
has arisen in part out of changes in the teaching of social
work, particularly from the influence of certain developments
in sociology as it has been taught to social workers, but also
through the contemporary teaching of such subjects as social
administration, philosophy, law and psychology. While
social work has traditionally relied on such contributions in
its claims to specialised knowledge, the new directions taken
by such disciplines have come as a disconcerting shock to
many social workers. The fact that reformist and activist
or radical segments are now represented in an important way
in the socialising programme is reflected by the controversy
among social work educators that has resulted. In a recent
paper on the expectations of teaching in social work courses
by the assistant director of CCETSW (CCETSW, 1977), some
of the more recent developments in social work training are
criticised, particularly the increasing influence of certain
macro-theories of a sociological kind. In some courses
this has displaced the student's learning of the skills that
are seen as basic to all social work. The purpose of social
work education is seen as the development of professional
skills, and the fostering of professional values, particularly

the idea that the main concern of the social worker was to
provide services to individual clients on a personal basis,
but that 'action to change social policy ... is political action
and outside the daily responsibility of the social worker'
(ibid.).

The responses to this document (CCETSW, 1979) provide
an interesting illustration of the nature of contemporary segmental affiliations in social work (although there is no way
of knowing how representative the responses are of all those
engaged in social work education). Probably the clearest
indication of this was the response to the proposition relating to professional values stated above. This drew the
greatest response of any of the original propositions, and
only a minority of respondents were in agreement with it.
The majority view, for example expressed by BASW, was
that social policies and their administration were the direct
concern of social workers because some clients' problems
were produced by the way policies are administered, or by
the policies themselves, thus emphasising the importance of
advocacy or brokerage roles. Some respondents went
further and emphasised that social work intervention was
itself a political matter and should be recognised as such.

While there are indications of highly polarised viewpoints
represented by widely differing segments, an interesting
feature of the arguments presented on both sides is the
appeal that is made to a variety of interests and a variety of
segmental affiliations. Although Wright (CCETSW, 1977) is
critical of the over-emphasis on macro-social science
approaches, he also points to courses in which there is a
lack of awareness of such factors. The critics of the original CCETSW paper also refer, apart from working within a
broad socio-economic context, to the importance of work with
individuals and families, although through a radically
changed form of practice. The appeal to a variety of segmental interests from members of a particular segment is a
form of manoeuvre so far given insufficient recognition in the
study of segmental behaviour.

(3) THE GENERIC/SPECIALIST CONTROVERSY

The second dichotomy of a less wide-ranging and more intra-
professional nature, though no less divisive in its consequences, is that of the conflict between the generic and
specialist principles in social work. Again, this struggle

was seen by the participants as having great significance
for the development of social work as a profession.

In chapter 3 the beginnings of the struggle to assert the
generic principle, in which importance is placed upon the
development of common social work knowledge and skills
irrespective of the settings in which these were used, was
traced.　This struggle began with the establishment at the
London School of Economics in 1954 of the first course
which was based upon the teaching of what were believed to
be the common elements in social work.　This development
has been described as a 'time bomb' in that it was bound to
have major, and probably to its progenitors, quite unexpected repercussions in part because of the dominance and
influence of the London School of Economics in social work
education at that time (Donnison, 1975).　But it was not until
some fifteen years later that the basis for the realisation of
the generic goal in practice was created with the unification
of separate local authority social work services into one
department (the probation service was still administratively
separate) and the consequent need for training to reflect
these new requirements.　It has been suggested that this
unification was unlikely to have been achieved without the
example of the generic courses that grew from the London
School of Economics model (ibid.).　But the intervening
period saw considerable conflict among a variety of interested parties, particularly the separate professional associations each representing different specialities and often with
long and distinguished histories.　These interests were also
expressed by social work educators, who stressed the
breadth of the new curriculum and the difficulty of doing
justice to the specific needs of client groups.　While many
were opposed to the generic idea, reflecting Hughes's (1958)
view of the tenacity with which pioneering teachers defend
the ground for which they have previously fought, the advantage of the new approach, in the words of one of its architects (Younghusband, 1978), was that

it broke down the walls of separation so that a qualified
social worker in one branch was not required to retrain
to become qualified in another and it demonstrated that
the common ground of casework was more fundamental than
the differences.

Just how powerful were the segmental and other affiliations
surrounding the generic debate is demonstrated by a case
study of the introduction of this course into the Department
of Social Science and Administration at the London School of

Economics (Donnison, 1975).   When the new generic course
was first introduced, it became the third separate social
work course in the department.   The differences between
the courses, while justifiable to some colleagues, were held
by others to involve irrational duplication of effort and waste
of scarce resources, particularly in competition for fieldwork placements.   Apart from disagreements within the
department, it was also necessary to recognise that the
status of social work education in the School was precarious,
and this was not helped by the existence of separate courses.
The new course claimed to introduce a wider range of skills
into the social work syllabus, including group and community
work, as well as a greater concern for social policy and
sociology.   The issue (although there were a number of
different versions of this) was the question of the integration of the three courses and how this was to be organised.
There was no agreement among the interested parties, which
included not only the teachers in the department, but fieldwork teachers and the agencies they represented as well as
training councils, over a considerable period of time.
Eventually, amalgamation of the courses did occur but not
without a lengthy period of conflict in which resolution was
brought about by appeal to higher and external authority.

The conflict not only underlines the difficulty of resolving
disputes among participants who feel that the conception they
have of the very nature of their profession is threatened,
but highlights the complexity of social work education itself,
particularly in its relationships to external and (in the last
resort) controlling interests.   As Donnison (1975) concludes:

> conflict of some kind was inevitable because the main par-
> ticipants were committed to conflicting objectives with the
> support of various groups outside the University whose
> divergent interests would have to break surface some-
> where, sooner or later.

It should be added that the debate about genericism is
still continuing, and the critics of this principle point to the
lack of specialised knowledge about specific client groups
(such as children and the mentally ill) among many social
workers, and the damaging consequences that this can have.

(4) ACCOMMODATION BETWEEN SEGMENTS

It is important to stress that the distinctions that have been made refer to a situation that is very complex; a particular complication is the likelihood that leaders in a profession may, in spite of the existence of deep division, emphasise unity and integration at particular points in time, for example when a profession is under external pressure or is a matter for public concern. Apart from this political form of 'fictional' unity, there is also no doubt that certain members of professions lay a stress on unity because of a genuine belief that professionals have enough in common to be only superficially divided on specific issues (this has been strongly argued in the case of psycho-therapy - see Storr, 1979). Again specialisms within a profession which have always traditionally been associated with a particular segment may in fact have much broader allegiances and interests. As Timms (1964) points out in his study of psychiatric social workers, there is no necessary connection between psychiatric social work and a therapeutic orientation: psychiatric social workers have shown a continuing interest in the reform of the law relating to children and young persons and the after-care of prisoners and have also argued against arbitrary distinction between therapy and reform. There was also evidence from the case studies in the research colleges of the acceptance and management of the conflict that was inherent in the two approaches, and certain elements which appeared basic to the standpoint of the reformist also appeared to be accepted in some senses by the therapist. An extract from Case Study B, whose reformist concern was not shared by the majority of her colleagues, illustrates the management of the conflict, and some of the consequences of the conflict for students:

Q: How do you see the relationship between your teaching and the rest of the course?

A: I think my teaching could be a bind for the rest of the course, it could set up a whole lot of conflicts. It could be very difficult but it hasn't been, and has fitted in very well on the whole. As a staff group we have discussed what we feel about this; everybody knows that I have reservations about casework and I don't pretend to have anything else, and this helps. One year there was a difficulty in that we had a group of students who split the staff; everything that was social administration was O.K. and everything that

was casework was awful. They did well on the social
administration paper and not on casework; never
happened before or since.
Q: Do you resolve this kind of problem?
A: Not sure we do; what happens in most years is that
most students see themselves as caseworkers but some
of them develop an interest in social administration and
may go off into different or allied fields, so that things
become complementary rather than antagonistic.

(5) CONCLUSION

It is clear that students face a complex variety of conflicting
expectations and influences from teachers, which often have
long histories and where the intensity of conflict changes
over time. Such conflicts will have their impact on the
selection of students, the structure of courses and the way
students are taught and assessed. Such conflicts are not
only matters for the course teachers and their students, but
involve external interests including the academic departments
and institutions in which courses are located and national
validating bodies, such as CCETSW and the CNAA. These
conflicts may seem less important to students than to
teachers, for the concern of the former is for survival and
success. In the case of the teachers, conflicts may be
accommodated and institutionalised by agreement to differ
and by the minimum requirements of actually running a
course. Most segments are represented in most training
schools and departments, although under certain circumstances it is possible for a segment to, in effect, capture a
particular training programme. Because of the tradition of
academic freedom, and the difficulty validating bodies have
in obtaining real information on day to day practice, there
will be considerable difficulty in mounting a successful
challenge to this particular form of professional authority.

Chapter six

Selection of students

(1) INTRODUCTION

Selection for entry to any profession has considerable significance for those who are selected, those who select and
for those who are rejected.   For those who are selected
the decision and the process leading to it means entry to the
first stages of a professional career and to preparation for
this career.   This may mean changes in the social status,
income, life-style and life chances of the candidate, in addition to membership of the professional community.   Entry to
professional training also implies the acceleration of a
period of adult socialisation and of change in the attitudes
and values of those undergoing this process.
     For the selectors the process of selection crystallises
their own professional attitudes and beliefs and their own
conceptions and images of the profession and its essential
work.   The selectors stand at the gateway of the profession
and select individuals who will be treated, in some cases
before the end of the training period, as professional
colleagues.   An essential element in training for the practising professions is that students work directly with clients
under supervision.   No matter how closely a student is
supervised, it is clear that certain responsibilities for the
client are exercised by the student.   As certain minimum
standards are required, it is important to exclude those
candidates who are unsuitable or unfit to practise as
students.   The search for the suitable candidate will be of
a rigorous nature, and this is some indication of the extent
to which a profession will attempt to obtain control over its
members.
     In the research courses the selection process started

some nine months before the next course actually began.
The analysis of applications, qualifications and references,
as well as the actual selection process in which candidates
are interviewed and observed in group situations, including
meetings between selectors to make final decisions, involves
a considerable expenditure of time and effort.   One estimate
is that this took up over 400 hours during a particular year;
258 hours were spent on interviews and 144 hours on staff
discussions following interviews (Ellis, 1975).

It is scarcely surprising that failure rates on certain professional training courses are low.   In social work the
wastage rates (including failure and withdrawal) for students
on CQSW courses (1973-9) varied from 3.3 to 4.6 per cent
(CCETSW, 1980b), compared to a rate of about 14 per cent
among undergraduate students (Robbins Report, 1963).

Selection is also surrounded by a series of dilemmas; one
of these is the conflict between the aim of maintaining high
standards and the pressure to train particular groups of
students, such as those sponsored by practice agencies or
who are recruited to meet increased demands for professional services at particular points in time.   There is also
the problem of those who fail to be selected for training.
The selectors may try to avoid conveying the impression that
their rejection of the candidate reflects on him in any general sense, or that he is unfitted for other professions.   In
social work strenuous attempts may be made to redirect or
counsel the unsuccessful to an extent which is rarely found
in other professions.

While selection is of the utmost importance in the professions, the actual process by which this occurs often appears
shrouded in mystery.   The situation might be likened to that
of a 'black box' (Coxon, 1965) where the inputs (or recruits)
can be fairly well described in terms of their social characteristics, and there is also similar information about the
outputs in terms of those who are actually recruited.   But
little is known about the actual process of selection and of
the interaction between selectors and candidates.

(2) AN APPROACH TO THE SELECTION PROCESS

One way of looking at the selection process is to see it as
one of the consequences of the character of the training
institution and its professional staff.   The professional
community and the dominant theories represented within it

will determine to a considerable extent what is looked for in candidates. A profession may be seen as a series of segments or groups of differing professional identities. Different segments may look for different characteristics in candidates and subject them to differing entrance tests. The survival of segments depends upon the recruitment of candidates who are potential successors and thus selection can be an important area of conflict in which segments attempt to select candidates who will aid survival, or attempt to gain control over selection procedures in general.

The training institution is also likely to be part of a larger administrative structure. The training programme may be financed and partly administered by a national or regional body. The training institution may have affiliations with other institutions or agencies and may use them as resources in the training programme; such institutions will be in contact with schools, hospitals, clinics and social work agencies. All these extra institutional influences are likely to enter the selection process and the socialisation programme through the training institution and its professional staff.

There will also be an approved and characteristic orbit through which candidates move on their way towards professional training. This includes certain academic and work experiences which it is believed will provide an adequate basis for professional training, and there will be informal links with other educational institutions as well as agencies in which the work of the profession is carried out and from which candidates may also be drawn. Candidates may apply as a result of being personally known to the selectors, for example as an untrained practitioner. Alternatively, training institutions may draw their candidates from a more or less unknown regional, or even national pool. Finally, each training institution will have a 'drawing power', based mainly on the reputation of the staff which will also influence potential candidates.

In a number of recent studies, the lack of clarity in the criteria for selection have been noted (Bucher and Stelling, 1977) and the situation is complicated by the fact that a certain amount of 'self selection' occurs among candidates who are shopping around to obtain places on particular courses. However, it is possible to set down what seems to be involved in getting accepted for a course and the kind of information sought by selectors and the means of obtaining this. There is also the question of conflict between the selectors over criteria for selection and how such conflicts are resol-

ved. The description that follows is drawn from a number
of accounts (including that of the author) of student selection
in social work, and is intended to suggest a general model
for the understanding of the selection process.

(3) INITIAL SELECTION PROCESS

The first hurdle faced by the prospective candidate is the
application form, with its demands for specific information
about the qualifications and experience of the applicant,
references and a detailed personal statement about the
candidate's interest in and motivation for social work. In
fact only 10 per cent of application forms sent out by the two
research courses were returned, an indication of the
demanding nature of the application form and its function as
an initial selective mechanism. Application forms are considered by the selectors* and certain candidates are called
for interview; 40 per cent of all applicants in Jones's (1970)
study were interviewed and about 50 per cent in the research
course.
   It is important, therefore, to note that a large number of
candidates are excluded on the documentary evidence submitted. In the research courses this kind of evidence was
used in a variety of ways, particularly as indicating a lack
of occupational and other experiences which are seen by the
selectors as a negative indication for selection. One form
of occupational experience which is viewed positively is
previous employment, or voluntary experience in social
work. Three-quarters of the candidates who were successful in the selection procedure for the research courses had
previous experience in social work. One avenue of recruitment has been for local authorities to appoint untrained
social workers with a view to their secondment to training
courses, although this policy is clearly at risk at a time of
cuts in local authority expenditure.

* The term 'selectors' refers to all those involved in the
selection process, whether in the initial screening process
or the interviews. Apart from the course tutors (social
workers) these may involve fieldwork teachers,
college lecturers and others; but as Jones (1970) comments
'under various guises the selection boards were on the
whole composed of social workers.'

One reason for this preference is to obtain some form of prior commitment to the profession and to test motivation. This may reflect a situation where training resources are scarce and the need to train very great. Obtaining prior commitment is both an indication of the suitability of the candidate through experience of the work of the profession, and also cuts wastage to a minimum.

For those with no previous experience in social work there is also a type of occupational experience approved by selectors and which is likely to lay the foundations for a successful application. This includes some form of occupational experience, or a sequence of such experiences, which lead to social work and contain elements which provide some preparation for social work as a career, so called 'bridging occupations' (Broom and Smith, 1967). The characteristics of such occupations include opportunities for resocialisation, or the redirection of the perspectives and aspirations of the individual, independency, or the dissociation of the individual from previous ties and commitments which might restrict mobility, and access to information and people which may assist the individual in movement into a desired occupation.

In the case of candidates for social work training there were a variety of 'bridging occupations', such as voluntary social work which gave candidates some idea of the nature of a 'helping relationship', provided a means by which they could compare this with previous work experiences and, perhaps most important of all, put them in touch with individuals who could sponsor them in the competition for entry to training by providing information about appropriate courses and career lines, as well as references.

Where such experiences were lacking, and the previous occupational record of the candidate did not appear to have social work as the end of a logical sequence, the candidate appeared at a distinct disadvantage. As one tutor to a research course put it 'we would be unimpressed with a candidate where the sequence of jobs doesn't seem to lead up to social work and it just seems the next thing to try out.' This is not the case in all professions; in nursing and health visiting an unstable employment record (so called 'touristry') is an accepted occupational trait and can be used in the selection process as a means of obtaining the maximum information about a candidate (Dingwall, 1977).

Another problem for the selectors is the question of the student's intellectual capacity. In the case of post-graduate

courses, such as the research university course, the
selectors are virtually assured of the candidate's intellectual capacities because of their previous experience of
higher education and possession of a degree or its equivalent.   One consequence of this is that attention can turn to
the candidate's motivation and personality.   While this is
important for all candidates, in the non-graduate courses
attention has to be given at the initial stage to basic educational qualifications or capacities because of the importance
of formal examinations in such courses.

   While the inquiry into the candidate's personal qualities
can be carried further at the interview stage, the candidate's personal statement is important in persuading the
selectors of his fitness or otherwise at this initial stage and
marks the beginning of the quest for the 'socially educable
student' (Towle, 1967).   As one tech tutor put it, 'personal
statements may sound more like psycho-social histories;
maybe the students we see later have as much pathology [as
those rejected on the basis of personal statements] but have
exercised more sensible judgement about it.'   Another tech
tutor put it more directly, 'we get applicants who are mentally sick, deprived in their own background; they are ruled
out.'   This highlights a major feature in the selection process in social work, the attempt to exclude those who are
unfitted on the grounds of some disabling aspect of the personality.   This is a particular problem for the counselling
professions for the candidate may see in a commitment to a
vocation such as social work (and as a result of contact with
the problems of others) the possibility of self-therapy and
self-realisation.   But from the professional point of view
the primary task is to offer a service to the client and one
function of the selection process is to insure the recruitment of candidates who can undertake these tasks.   Yet
there is a major confusion in professional social work thinking at this point, which stems from the tendency to describe,
explain and interpret social work (including occupational
choice) in therapeutic and particularly psycho-analytic
terms (Pearson, 1973).   For example, the desire to help
can be interpreted as an individual's guilt in the face of
social problems, in which it is phantasised that the self has
played a part, and for which reparation is being attempted
through entry to social work.   Images of motivation include
the 'rescue complex' of the child-care worker, and the
desire of the psychologically insecure to have clients dependent on them.   But less often are accounts given of occupa-

tional choice in terms of the untutored motivation of the raw
recruit, which typically blend a simple desire to help with
the realistic aim of self—completion and personal development, although the candidate may learn to present only
certain aspects of his motivations to the selectors.   Thus
professional accounts of candidates' motivation bear little
relation to that of recruits and often function negatively to
highlight motives which disqualify rather than those which
are positive indications for entry to training.

(4) FINAL SELECTION PROCESS

A personal appearance before the selectors constitutes the
final stage of the selection process, either in the form of an
individual interview (usually with a social work tutor and
sometimes another teacher) or a selection board or both (in
Jones's 1970 study all candidates were given a board but only
two-thirds an individual interview).   Some selectors also
make use of other methods of obtaining information about
candidates – including psychological or other forms of testing and a group discussion among candidates which is observed by the selectors.

Until recently the use of the interview in selection for
social work has gone almost unchallenged.   The main reason
for the use of the interview has been the 'special need to
test the applicant's capacity for personal relationships
before he enters professional education for social work'
(Edwards, 1971).   Another purpose is to enable the candidate to get as much information as possible about social
work and the training institution.

The selectors on the research courses also believed that
it was important to test a candidate's capacities for personal
relationships:

University tutor: One looks for comeback – is this the
kind of person I like talking to and from
which something comes back.

Tech tutor: If you get no feeling that they are making a
real relationship with you, you get the feeling
that they are not for the field.

Tech tutor: It depends if I get on with them; if someone
withdraws completely, is unable to give out
anything from themselves, one would be
worried.

But there was also a more concrete purpose to the inter-

view, a further exploration of the candidate's life history
based upon the personal statement, including the experience
of early childhood, later family and work experiences,
experiences of and reactions to stress in family and work
situations, illness of both mental and physical kinds and
bereavement. Here the attempt to distinguish between
those seen as 'fit' or 'unfit' for practice is continued. One
test of fitness is reactions to stressful situations or problems the individual has faced in his life and rather than
looking for candidates with uneventful or unstressful lives,
selectors appeared to emphasise certain reactions to stress
of a positive nature which had led to growth in the personality.

> Tech tutor: It is important to know how the candidate had
> come through stress; maybe that somebody
> who had come through would make a better
> social worker than those with unstressful
> lives.

> University tutor: The fact that a student had had personal
> experience of stress wouldn't preclude
> acceptance /for the course/ if it seemed
> he had potential for social work.

These statements closely parallel the findings of Bucher
and Stelling (1977) in their study of psychiatric training.
Here the candidates did not necessarily have to be mentally
'healthy'; the question was whether they could stand up to
emotional stress. One reason for rejecting candidates was
because they were too well defended, although how such
judgments were made by the selectors must in the words of
Bucher and Stelling 'be classified as a clinical art'.

In practice, between a third and a half of the research
course candidates who were interviewed were, according to
the selectors, generally suitable for training, on the basis
of the criteria suggested above. There were, therefore, a
number of further considerations dictating the final choice.
Although the candidate is adjudged as suitable for training
he may not be suitable for this particular course. The
urgency of the candidate's need to train may also vary.
For example, in situations where the candidate is already
in social work, some agencies may be providing adequate
in-service training while others are not. Finally, candidates are also selected to fit in with the requirements of the
teaching method. In both research courses much of the
teaching is carried out in small seminar groups of between
10 and 15 people and these need to be balanced in terms of

the sex and age composition of the group and the experience of group members.   The necessity to recruit on the basis of these factors will have an influence on the final selection of candidates.   Finally, candidates were also judged in terms of whether they would make students who were 'acceptable' to their teachers;   one of the final questions the selectors on the research courses put to themselves was 'would we be prepared to tutor or supervise this person?'

(5)   AN INTERPRETATION OF THE SELECTION PROCESS

According to Towle (1967) the socially educable student is one 'who can become motivated to work for the common good rather than be driven largely to strive for self maximation or for the maximation of those who, closely related in his life situation, are an extension of himself.'   Another element is the capacity of the candidate to use the actual educational process as a means to personal maturation and growth, aside from a display of intellectual excellence.   As indicated, this does not imply the exclusion of those whose progress through life has been eventful, even stressful, rather the desire is to choose those who have responded positively to problems and challenges and who have through their responses shown signs of personal growth and insight.   In their search for the 'socially educable' candidate the selectors placed little weight upon factors such as academic performance, or formal tests of intelligence, personality or educational attainment.   Instead, they turned to a method with which they themselves were most familiar in their own practice, an approach   which concentrates on the biography and personality of the individual and his mode of 'presentation of self'. Importance was attached to the candidate's personal statement and to the presentation of the self of the candidate to the selectors during the final phase of the selection process. There are a number of reasons for the importance attached to the candidate's presentation of self.   Towle (1967), discussing the comparative advantages of the written autobiography and the selection interview, criticises the former (which has come to be used in selection by certain American schools of social work because in many cases candidates and schools are separated by vast distances) on the grounds that it is written to a fantasy person.   This does not give an adequate guide to the candidate's capacities for understanding or relating to others: 'the decisive point is that the

autobiography is not an interview and cannot substitute for
it ... it approximates the sociologist's questionnaire, an
instrument with which the social caseworker is not at home'
(ibid.).

Again, during the selection process the candidate cannot
actually be observed playing the role of the professional and
participating in the work of the profession.   But social work
educators see the selection process as itself providing the
means for testing the candidate for a future professional
role.   The candidate is observed at the start of the pursuit
of a distant goal and his responses to the obstacles and
problems met with during the selection process, which is a
stressful situation in which the student is asked to adjust to
a variety of different demands and circumstances (interviews,
tests, group situations), can be observed.   The way in
which the candidate reacts to the challenge of a distant goal
may be predictive of his reactions to goals in professional
work.   Again the candidate must submit to a rigorous test of
his motivations both verbally and in writing and the challenge
of this situation will effectively test his defences and capacities for adaptation.   According to Towle one kind of adaptation (and presumably an acceptable one from the professional
point of view) centres around the realistic acceptance of the
selection process by the adoption of a questioning and partially independent stance;   alternatively, the candidate may
submit absolutely and unquestioningly to the process in pursuit of a neurotic desire to attain his goal at any price.

Clearly there are differences in the emphasis laid upon
different elements in the selection process, between the life
history of the candidate compared to a picture of him in the
present, or on the exact focus of the inquiry into the self of
the candidate.   But until recently there has been considerable agreement among social workers about the kind of
selection procedure which is appropriate (Ellis, 1975).

In spite of this, criticisms of the selection process have
grown and the outline of an alternative set of ideas about
selection has appeared.   The main grounds of criticisms are
the evidence that is used as the basis of decisions, both of a
documentary kind and the results of interviews.   Thus a
large number of candidates is excluded on documentary evidence alone.   This raises the issue of the adequacy of this
evidence and the question of whether some of these candidates would have proved suitable had they been interviewed.
The main basis of exclusion at this stage apart from educational and other standard criteria were candidates' biog-

raphies and personal statements which provided, among
other things, case history material on the candidate, such
as evidence of previous involvement in voluntary social work.
   Although previous involvement in voluntary work might be
evidence of motivation towards social work and of capacities
to form professional rather than 'need' relationships, it is
not necessarily the most important indication of suitability
to train (Jones, 1970).   The interview has also come under
increasing criticism, not only because it is time-consuming
but because of its unsatisfactory predictive qualities and
because it may be more unfair to the candidates than the
assessment of documentary evidence.   For example, research suggests that interviewers tend to make up their
minds about an applicant early in the interview and that
lengthy interviews do not materially affect their decision
(Mayfield, 1964; cited in Ellis, 1975), while interviewers
might be impressed by candidates whose management of self
was good enough to hide deficiencies that would emerge in
other situations (Ellis, 1975).
   In one of the few pieces of research designed to test the
usefulness of the interview as a selective device, the success rates of students at Middlesex Polytechnic selected on
the basis of written application only and by written application and interview were compared (Edwards and Foster,
1980).   The interview was not a significant factor in pre-
dicting success on the course, which was similar for both
groups.   However, while the study demonstrated that suitable candidates can be selected without interview, those
selected on the basis of written application alone were less
likely to accept a place on the course.
   Research by Ellis (1975) at Birmingham also indicated
that interview decisions are not necessarily superior to
pre-interview assessments and are not a uniquely valuable
selective instrument.   The rationality of interviews as a
selective mechanism has attracted considerable criticism
over a number of years, but there is little evidence that the
importance of the interview in selection for social work is
being seriously challenged.
   A major reason for criticising a reliance on the presentation of self of the candidate is that the candidate (particularly in the interview situation) can learn that the selection
system is in reality a kind of game which, if the rules are
known, can be played out to the approval of the selectors.
Thus according to one American researcher (Shey, 1968),
the candidate or student is out

to play the game – whether or not this is reality does not matter. He wants to be seen as psychically fit, i.e. emotionally stable and mature and to believe that his reasons for wanting to work with people are legitimate, born of something other than purely personal needs.

The selection process may, in professions such as social work, have a significance which far outweighs the selection choice of likely candidates for training. This is suggested by studies which show that the socialisation process in social work occurs not so much during formal training and education, but before and after this period. Thus Hayes and Varley (1968) showed that the degree of change in values between entering and graduating students is limited and that the greatest change in values occurs after graduation and during work experience and not durimg the schooling period.

One explanation is that it is the admissions process as such which replaces the socialisation process of the school; thus most candidates for admission have already had experience in social work prior to their applications and are already partially socialised in that they have been exposed to some of the values of the profession (Landsberg, 1967). The selection process, being of a rigorous and demanding nature, serves to select out those whose values are congruent with those of the profession. This leaves far less to be accomplished by formal socialisation than might otherwise be thought. In addition, the student becomes acquainted with the experiences he is likely to undergo on the course and with the educational process that is to follow, and the admissions process can be seen in some ways as a model of this educational process and of what is to follow in the career of the professional social worker. For this and other reasons, the issues surrounding selection for social work are crucial to a profession where the battle for professional status is far from won.

The so-called Vyas case highlights some of these issues, particularly the conflict between professional and bureaucratic authority. The case concerned an education welfare officer employed by a local authority who applied for admission to a CQSW course (similar to the tech course being described here) in a polytechnic. The local authority in question, which supported his application, was also partly responsible for financing the polytechnic and its social work course. The applicant was at first admitted without going through the normal selection process but after protests from

teaching staff, went through the normal selection process
and was rejected as unsuitable for social work training.
His employers reacted by reducing financial support for the
polytechnic and this was restored only after the reservation
of 5 places on the course for education welfare officers
employed by the authorities financing the polytechnic. The
applicant was eventually admitted to the course after further
pressure from the local authority, but the CCETSW deci-
ded to take the case to the High Court. Judgment was
announced in May 1978 (Times Law Report, 4 May 1978) to
the effect that the methods by which the selection decision
was arrived at were less than fully fair to the applicant,
including the discussions with the candidate at a later interview of the circumstances of his rejection at an earlier
stage. The importance of this practice in selection for
social work was not something that was considered in court,
but the court did not deny the discretion of educational
institutions in the admission of students (Parsloe, 1979).
    While it would be straining the imagination too far to
believe that local authorities in these circumstances would
not legitimately claim some interest in the admission of their
employees to training courses, the question at issue is
whether this claim amounts to the right of admission. This
would imply a challenge to the right of a profession to
authority over admission to training. But the situation is
further complicated by the fact that bureaucracies and professions share certain forms of procedure and the values
underlying such forms. As Parsloe (1979) argues, while a
central precept of selection has been challenged in this
decision and thus implicitly the right of a profession to act
autonomously, concern that the individual be treated fairly
and in terms of 'natural justice' (including the possibility
that the reasons for failure to be selected should be
explained to a candidate) is also a concern clearly shared
by social work itself. The conflict between professional
and bureaucratic practices revealed by the Vyas case and
the form in which this was resolved seems to indicate the
role of administrative rationality in the resolution of such
conflict – that is, a set of shared principles which are
common to both professional and bureaucratic procedures.

Chapter seven

Social characteristics of students

(1) INTRODUCTION

What kind of students successfully survive the selection process and are recruited to social work training? What changes have there been in the characteristics of students in the recent past? The importance of information on such areas as age, sex, class and previous occupational and educational experience is twofold. It is important in a profession which has experienced rapid change to assess changes in patterns of recruitment so that they can be set alongside the overt objectives both of the training programmes and of practice in general. One objective in the development of social work has been the desire to extend the services of social workers to a wider spectrum of the population, but also to recruit new workers from a greater variety of social groups (Seebohm Report, 1968).

It is also important to know whether differences in social characteristics influence students' progress through the socialising programme. Part of the complexity of the socialising process lies in the different ways in which students experience training, and it is important to assess the influence of basic demographic characteristics on this experience. This implies the interaction between the past or biographical world of the student and that of the present when the individual is faced with new situations to which he has to respond. Such biographies are a feature of any situation met with in the present and a resource for dealing with that situation. They form both 'structural' or continuing elements in any situation, but their use will also be determined by specific features of that situation (Schutz and Luckmann, 1974). One typical situation faced by students

on professional courses is that of being placed in an
'incompetent' or learner status, something made even more
difficult by the fact that such students are adults and are
thus otherwise held to be 'competent' members of the wider
society. The problem is made worse for the older students
because they, unlike their younger counterparts, are no
longer familiar with situations in which 'learning the ropes'
is a normal and expected component of everyday life. It is,
rather, part of the experience and expectations of the young.
Some educational institutions and professions have attempted
to solve this problem by segregating older students on
'special' or 'emergency' courses in which an attempt is made
to treat such students as adults rather than students.

Social work students come from diverse social backgrounds, but the majority do share one experience which is
important in their present situation as students – the vast
majority have previous experience of social work in one
form or another. Virtually all (98.3 per cent) entrants to
one-year post-graduate courses in England and Wales in
1975 (Collison and Kennedy, 1977) had previous experience
of paid or voluntary social work (and many had extensive
experience) and two-thirds were seconded from an employer.
In Parsloe and Stevenson's 1979 study 95 per cent of students in the 6 courses studied had previous local authority
experience and two-thirds were seconded. In the research
courses nearly three-quarters of the students had previous
experience of regular social work employment and two-thirds
were seconded. The implication of this is that social work
students may be more sceptical and critical about their training experiences than other professional students, but may
also face the problem of having not only their adult competence but their previous competence as members of the occupation called into question. These factors are a recipe for
an educational environment which may be unusually diverse,
complex and fraught with conflict.

(2) SEX

The intake to all CQSW courses in 1979 showed a 62:38 per
cent female/male distribution (CCETSW, 1980a). There
were considerable variations among courses; for example
on the one-year post-graduate course 67 per cent of students were female (in Collison's 1975 study the figure was
also 70 per cent) compared to 58 per cent on the two-year

non-graduate courses. In the research courses, the
university post-graduate course had a similarly high percentage of women, but the two-year tech course had an
equal balance of males and females. The proportion of
males entering social work training increased during the
1950-60 period from 20 to 33 per cent (Jones, 1964). Since
then the two-year non-graduate courses have provided an
additional avenue for male recruitment. Collison and
Kennedy (1977) suggest, however, that this trend may have
been reversed and that women are tending to re-establish
their traditional position in social work.

(3) AGE

The average age of the 1975-6 entrants to graduate one-year
courses was 26.4 (ibid.) and for the students in the research
courses 26.0. This is some indication of the late age entry
to social work training, compared to occupations such as
nursing and teaching. There are, however, variations
between courses; while over 76 per cent of the students on
one- and two-year post-graduate courses are between 20 and
30, the two-year non-graduate course has a much wider age
distribution, with 53 per cent between 20 and 30 but 30 per
cent between 30 and 40 and 16 per cent over 40 (CCETSW,
1980a). Apart from the post-graduate status of one part of
social work education, the late age of entry to training is
also explained by the emphasis placed by the selectors of
students on previous experience in social work.

(4) SOCIAL CLASS

Social work students (classified by father's occupation) are
like all students in higher education heavily over represented
in professional (class I) and intermediate or semi-professional (class II) occupations: overall these occupations
account for nearly 60 per cent of the 1975 university
entrants and 52 per cent of research course students compared to 23 per cent of the general population (see Table
7.1). Altogether students with middle-class (non-manual)
origins made up 74 and 61 per cent of the two groups of students compared to 35 per cent of the general population. A
rather similar pattern emerges when social workers in the
field are considered (see Table 7.1) although the distribution

TABLE 7.1 Social class of social work students, clients and workers (%)

Social class	Students		Social workers			Clients	
	University one year post-graduate 1975–6	Research courses 1969–70	Bucks 1960–1	Bradford 1967–8	Bucks	Bradford	England and Wales
I Professional etc. occupations	22.2	13.1	17.9	7.1	16.0	2.0	5.0
II Intermediate occupations	37.7	39.0	44.6	31.3		6.4	18.2
III Skilled occupations (non-manual)	14.1 / 74.0	9.5 / 61.6	62.5	52.5	47.0	52.6	12.1 / 35.3
III Skilled occupations (manual)	17.2	19.3	37.5				38.3
IV Partly skilled occupations	7.3	15.3		6.1	37.0	24.3	17.0
V Unskilled occupations	1.5 / 26.0	3.8 / 38.4	37.5	3.0 / —	—	14.7 / —	8.4 / 63.7

in Bradford is nearer that of the country as a whole than the
figures for the other groups. By comparison clients present an opposite picture, under-represented in the middle-
class groups and over-represented among manual workers,
although 16 per cent of clients in Bucks and 6 per cent in
Bradford were in professional or semi-professional occupations.

There were also a number of variations in class origins.
In the research courses 45 per cent of tech students had
manual working-class origins compared to 30 per cent of
university post-graduate students (a proportion close to
that for all such students in Collison's 1975 study). Among
tech students, 22 per cent had skilled and 19 per cent had
semi-skilled manual origins. This suggests that courses
outside the universities may attract a more balanced class
intake and be an important source for the widening of the
class origins of social workers.

The social origins of male and female social workers also
differ (see Table 7.2). Of the women in Collison's study,
77 per cent had middle-class origins (24 per cent of them in
class I) compared to 66 per cent of men (17 per cent in class
I). In the research courses 75 per cent of women compared to 45 per cent of men had middle-class origins; 4
per cent of men and 21 per cent of women had class I
origins. In Jefferys's (1965) study of social workers in
Bucks, 65 per cent of females compared to 55 per cent of
males had middle-class origins. Among American social
work students, 75 per cent of females against 59 per cent of
males had middle-class origins (Pins, 1967).

(5) EDUCATION

Of Collison's 1975 group of students, 80 per cent had as
their highest qualification a degree or post-graduate degree
of some kind. The post-graduate students in the research
courses had a similar educational background, but by sharp
contrast over a quarter of the research tech students had
left school (sometimes as early as 14) with no formal qualifications or 1 or 2 GCE 'O' level passes. They were thus
entering social work education with little or no previous
formal education. But over half of the research tech students had 5 or more GCE 'O' levels and a quarter had 2 or
more 'A' levels, that is minimum university entrance qualifications. This latter group comprised younger people who

TABLE 7.2 Social class origin of male and female students and social workers (%)

		All university one year post-graduate social work students 1975-6		All research students 1969-70		Bucks social workers 1960-1	
		Males	Females	Males	Females	Males	Females
I	Professional	17.0	24.3	4.2	21.4	6.2	22.2
II	Semi professional	30.8	40.6	25.0	50.0	49.0	43.3
III	Skilled non-manual	18.9	12.1	16.6	3.6		
	Total non-manual	66.7	77.0	45.8	75.0	55.2	65.5
III	Skilled manual	20.1	16.0	33.4	7.2		
IV	Semi skilled manual	12.6	5.2	16.6	14.2	44.8	34.5
V	Unskilled	0.6	1.8	4.2	3.6		
	Total manual	33.3	23.0	54.2	25.0	44.8	34.5

were frequently unsuccessful 'A' level or university candidates or university dropouts.   They were generally younger
than those with fewer formal qualifications.   For these
students, social work often seemed an occupation of second
choice, as well as an opportunity of a college education
which would otherwise be denied, an indication that career
choice is sometimes the result of fortuitous and paradoxical
circumstances rather than a direct and conscious progression towards a chosen end.   This group of research tech
students therefore varied considerably in their age, class
and educational background compared to the university students.   Of the graduates in Collison's study, about three-
quarters had a previous academic education in sociology
and/or social administration, while only 5.8 per cent listed
psychology as their undergraduate subject.

(6) ORIGINS AND MOTIVATIONS

One of the most important issues raised by a consideration
of the social characteristics of social work students is that
of changing class origins.   The social origins of social
work students as a whole are becoming more diverse; in
spite of the image of social work as a mainly middle-class
profession the recent developments in training have provided
an avenue for the recruitment of workers whose origins are
closer to the majority of their clients than the previous,
mainly university trained corps of workers.   While only
26 per cent of Collison's 1975 intake to university post-
graduate courses were children of manual workers (and a
similar percentage in the university research course), over
44 per cent of the students on the research tech course had
manual origins.   In Jefferys's (1965) study of social
workers in Buckinghamshire, the proportions with working-
class origins rose from 12 per cent for medical and psychiatric social workers with professional training to 39 per cent
for those who are untrained.   As this latter group would
provide the main reservoir from which those entering two-
year, non-graduate courses would come, it seems reasonable to suppose that this will mean a trend in the direction of
increasing proportions of social workers with working-class
origins, a factor left out of account in Collison's study of
the background of university-trained social workers, who
will eventually work alongside students trained in other
institutions and courses.   One issue raised by this is that

social work is an occupation which can offer, for those with working-class or lower-middle-class origins, a rise in occupational status and therefore represents an avenue of upward social mobility. In these terms, nearly half of all the research students (and nearly 60 per cent of tech students) will be moving up in social status on becoming social workers.

One of the consequences of this situation for the socialisation process is that for a sizeable number of students this process can be viewed not only as an introduction to a particular occupational setting but also as an entry to a new social status. Thus, for some students, the learning and teaching situation, the development of specifically professional relationships with clients, contacts with tutors, other teachers and supervisors, can all be viewed as initial contacts with a new middle-class professional world and with middle-class norms and values. Although the majority of students had experience of social work before the course, the training course itself, with its emphasis on the growth of the student's 'professional identity', 'deferred gratification' and other middle-class traits and with traditional and recognisable professional figures (such as lawyers, doctors and psychiatrists) playing some of the leading roles, is a much more powerful evocation of the professional occupational life that is to follow than that represented by the social work agency and by experience of practice alone.

It is also clear that a desire to improve social and occupational positions was one of the motivations for entry to social work. In the author's original research a distinction was made between the 'instrumental' and 'expressive' elements of the choice of a social work career. In the former, action is oriented towards the achievement of some goal or state of affairs in the future, which will not come about without the intervention of the actor in the course of events: immediate gratifications are renounced in favour of the greater gains resulting from the attainment of some goal. Correspondingly, 'expressive' action is not oriented to the achievement of some future goal but to 'the organisation of the "flow" of gratifications' in the present (Parsons, 1951). Both represent situations in which actors give different types of primacy to particular kinds of interests and actions. For the instrumentalist, career choice is oriented to the attainment of material rewards or status, rewards that are mainly extrinsic to the career in question. The expressive actor values particular components of a given career for the intrinsic satisfaction they can provide. Two-thirds of tech students (compared with about two-fifths of university students) expressed their career choice in a broadly instrumental fashion, ranging from a direct emphasis on the opportunity of upward mobility that social work provided to those who stressed the inadequacies of previous occupations and the advantages, such as variety, autonomy and security, that social work can offer.

The two extracts which follow illustrate the extremes of these two categories of instrumental and expressive career choice. The first represents the views of a 27-year-old tech student. Previously he was a clerk in local authority for 7 years. He has 3 'O' levels; his father is a clerical worker:

Knew nothing about social work but realised (when working in local authority) that could become a social worker; always fairly ambitious - it was getting on rather than being a social worker, didn't want to be a clerk all my life. From first day I was in local government chap said to me 'only way to get on is to move on'. Absolutely by chance a job came up in the health and welfare department.

The second represents the views of a 22-year-old female graduate on the university course. She has no work experience; her father is a minister of religion:

Wanting to help, didn't want to be a social reformer though my parents were religious, father a missionary. Had dreams of being a missionary. My school also had a strong social conscience.

There have been a number of attempts to trace the implications of a rise in social status for the individuals involved, one of which is the conflict between the attitude and values of the class of origin and that into which movement is taking place. This had been a theme of a number of studies of mobility, including Jackson and Marsden's 1962 study of the careers of working-class children at grammar schools. Although this interpretation has been much criticised, it does suggest that the recent recruits to a social work career and a middle-class status may wish to consolidate their new status rather than to use it as a springboard for critical or activist concerns in relation to their chosen occupations. Cypher (1975) has in fact defined the profile of the social work activist as including middle-class origins, a university social science degree and in the younger age group. The recent recruits to social work training in the non-university sector constitute a group which largely differs from this

general picture. They may be nearer the status-conserv-
ing and largely middle-of-the-road teachers who were the
products of some of the grammar schools in the 1960s
(Jackson and Marsden, 1962).

Chapter eight

Role playing and role models

(1) INTRODUCTION: PLAYING THE ROLE

It has long been recognised that playing the role of the professional during training is of key importance in the socialisation process. An important part of what happens to people as they move through a socialising programme is to undertake the work of the profession and be assessed on their performance. But the impact of training could be very different if students are merely 'playing at' role playing (Bucher and Stelling, 1977). Real role playing involves making important decisions and having responsibility and accountability for the actions taken. For example, in the early years of medical school, students are mainly going through the motions, although there may be times when real responsibilities are thrust upon them. By comparison, social work students are normally asked, almost from the start of their practical training, to take responsibility for clients. While supervisors may be stage managing this work, students may still feel they are really playing professional roles. Other properties of the role-playing situation include the degree of clarity and consensus among teachers over the roles to be played and the range and centrality of roles. If trainees are unclear about what is being asked of them then role playing will have less impact; this may arise when staff are not agreed on what is the real work of the profession or are offering conflicting models of practice. The range of roles the trainee is offered may vary. For example, these may be limited to certain areas of practice at the expense of other important areas. Again, trainees may undertake roles which are highly valued in the profession or ones which are peripheral.

(2) ROLE PLAYING IN SOCIAL WORK EDUCATION

Social work students do actually experience something of
the reality of practice during their training.   Students,
during their work in social work agencies, do make important decisions and take responsibility for their actions and,
though the ultimate responsibility lies with the fieldwork
teacher, this experience appears none the less real.   Students work with clients of the agency and offer them its services and it is somewhat difficult for the role of student
within this setting to be institutionalised or for the work of
the student to be segregated from that of the agency in spite
of the existence in some agencies of specialised student
units set up for training purposes.   If this were not the
case it would imply crucial variations in the service given
by the agency.   As Timms (1970) remarks 'the agency ...
does not exist only to help in the training of social workers,
and the work of the student must for administrative as well
as educational reasons not be allowed to fall below the bare
minimum of competence.'   The role of student is thus not
one which is emphasised to the client public and students in
the research courses did not find it necessary to explain
their role.   The definition of the role of student
in the agency is thus one of practitioner and this is one
reason why it is difficult to dilute the responsibility of
trainees in playing roles of key importance.
     In the research courses students were introduced to the
realities of practice early on in their agency placements.
Apart from short periods at the beginning of each course
where they spent some time as observers in everyday situations, from almost the beginning of their courses students
dealt directly with clients and assumed (under supervision)
responsibilities for their actions in relation to clients.   No
more dramatic indication of this form of reality can be given
than the example of students working alongside other social
workers in ghetto situations (Mayer and Rosenblatt, 1975).
Here not only were the limits set by the school to the extent
of the exposure of students to the dangers of ghetto situations somewhat amorphous, but students felt they had to
persevere in these situations because their performance was
being evaluated and the outcome of their final assessment
was heavily dependent on receiving a favourable supervisory
appraisal.   Because of the difficulty in assessing the effectiveness of the student as a helping person, his sheer stick-
ing power in extreme situations becomes all the more important.

Another indication of the reality or otherwise of the role-playing situation is in students' perceptions of whether the training course is an adequate preparation for the real work of the profession. In Parsloe and Stevenson's (1978) account of CQSW courses students felt adequately trained (that is, scored well when adequacy was rated) in areas (such as family relationships) which were thought of as important in the work of the social work practitioner. Adequacy scores for areas in which there was a lower expectation of work (such as community groups) were much lower. There was in general a feeling that students were adequately trained for their subsequent work.

The main threat to the reality of role playing is supervision. Social work is characterised, along with many similar occupations, by the degree to which the student (and also the practitioner) is supervised in his work. Supervision will, for the student, be a matter of the utmost importance and will lie at the core of the student's learning process. What happens during supervision will vary from one setting to another and between courses, and different models for the administration of fieldwork teaching exist (Pettes, 1979).

Students on the research courses reported that although they were closely supervised during their initial placement, they were given an increasing amount of autonomy as the course progressed. One university student on looking back at his training said that he 'was very dependent in first placement – scarcely took a decision without consulting supervisor – in Probation entirely on own, one weekly supervision.' Another university student related a similar experience: 'much closer supervision in first placement – all my records looked at in Child Care; now supervision is what I want, can ask for something to be discussed when I want it.'

One reason for variations in the amount of supervision, apart from the increasing experience and confidence of students, was differences in the setting of the agency. Agencies which were involved in statutory services which required the application of statutory regulations, clearly involved more supervision (particularly in the initial stages of training) than agencies where this did not apply, particularly voluntary settings.

But the possibility of over supervision is still present, implying that students are protected from reality and that their activities and decisions are stage managed by supervi-

sors. This problem was voiced by some students in the
DHSS study (Parsloe and Stevenson, 1978) where the implications of some students' comments were that they were not
sufficiently in touch with the realities of the local authority
setting in which they worked. A number of fieldwork
teachers in some local authorities stressed a model of
social work practice which was at variance with that typical
of the employing authority. This contributed to a belief
among students that placements had not in all circumstances
prepared them adequately for the work they would be doing
after qualification.

Another aspect of this situation is that students are not
always made aware of the constraints under which they and
the agency are operating (such as lack of resources) and
tend to blame themselves for 'failures' in their practice
(Mayer and Rosenblatt, 1974). But the problem may also
arise from the kind of cases made available by the agency
for students to work on. Students have criticised the limited opportunities made available to student units by certain
agencies (Curnock, 1975).

A second type of conflict that may have implications for
the reality of role playing by students is that between the
college and practice settings. While both are staffed by
social workers, the college tutors have transferred to an
academic setting and, although they may try to keep in
touch with practice, exercise their primary task as teachers.
The supervisors have an educational role to play vis à vis
students but their responsibilities are primarily to their
employing agency. This is clearly the basis of conflict
between college and agency, and there is evidence that students felt they were in a conflict situation within the agency,
although the unity of college and agency is often stressed as
a basic organisational and ideological feature of training
(Davies, 1979a).

A particular feature of this conflict emerges from Parsloe
and Stevenson's (1978) study. A number of college teachers
(both social workers and others) were negative in their
attitude to the local authority in which the student was
placed or would enter after training. Social work tutors
commented adversely on the prospect: 'the local authority
scene is gloomy beyond belief and we can't in all conscience
fit people for that'; and 'negativism is the only possible
attitude. The students are going back to this being trodden
on from a great height.'

There was little attempt to help the student to cope with

such negative attitudes and only a minority of the teachers
had experience themselves of working in such structures.
The part-time work in which some of them were involved
was mainly in voluntary agencies or hospitals in which the
pattern of work is very different from local authorities.
The evidence used by such teachers to form their view of
local authorities was thus usually secondhand and mediated
through students and supervisors. Again, there was a lack
of more general contact between the courses and local
authorities – for example, most contact was with supervisors and other training staff, and there were few contacts
with management or research and development departments.
Social work teachers were therefore most often associated
with a marginal aspect of the local authority, and did not
have a full view of wider aspects of their work.

In the research courses the 'core act' (an activity or
a class of activities embodying the basic skill and mission
of the occupation or segment (Bucher and Stelling, 1977))
for which the students were being prepared seemed to be
based upon work with individuals and their families within
the tradition of social casework and the casework relationship between social worker and client. The experiences
of students as they progressed through training programmes
illustrate the importance of this definition of the core act.
Near the outset of their training the definition of social
work among the majority of students was variously given
as: 'a general helping relationship'; 'helping specific
groups of people'; and 'help involving material or financial aid'. By the end of their course, a much greater
consensus had emerged among students and 9 out of 10 of
them were agreed that social work was based primarily
on 'the understanding of individual feelings and
emotions'.

Although alternative definitions of the core act were
available, they found only limited expression among this
group of students. This type of definition also reflects the
historical circumstances which had produced the social
work teachers of that time. Thus, settings such as medical
and psychiatric social work had a strong influence over the
definitions of the social work role and methods at this time.
The focus was very much on the relationships between client
and worker, and an appreciation of the constraints of a particular setting tended to stress psychological factors rather
than practical constraints (Parsloe and Stevenson, 1978).

Although this form of definition of the core act has

retained some of its importance, the general situation has
undergone considerable change. This is well illustrated by
Parsloe and Stevenson's study in which alternative definitions of the 'task of the social worker in relation to direct
work with individuals and families' were presented to students who were asked to choose between them. The choices
lay between a focus on (1) 'any area of the lives of individuals and families which appears to be creating the greatest
difficulties for their clients'; (2) a concern to help 'individuals and families get a fairer deal from the various social
institutions upon which they depend'; and (3) a primary concern to help 'individuals and their families, through a relationship, to understand and to modify or resolve their difficulties'. To simplify, the three approaches were defined
as 'integrated', 'sociological' and 'psychological', the
latter bearing a strong resemblance to the type of core act
identified in the research courses some ten years before.
Of the students, 63 per cent chose the integrated definition,
10 per cent the sociological and 27 per cent the psychological, indicating a considerable shift of emphasis between the
two groups of students. The main differences between the
different approaches were that the sociological group was
more interested in community work and work with offenders
than the others and the psychological group was more interested than others in work with the sick and disabled. In
all groups there was a high level of interest in work with
families and children. There was some lack of stability in
these definitions when students were followed up into practice, indicating a situation of considerable fluidity in the
meanings attached to different definitions.
  The potential for conflict between different approaches,
particularly between the sociological and psychological
models, poses a threat to the successful experience of
role playing in the courses and may lead to the adoption
of rigid and entrenched positions, a situation that has not
been entirely resolved by the adoption of the integrated
approach as a bridge between conflicting definitions.
The following extract (anon., 1968), although dating from
the late 1960s, illustrates well the difficulties a student
experiences who comes to a social work course with a
background in sociology:
  The sociological approach can conflict with that of the
  social worker who is primarily interested in needs and
  problems of the individual. Graduates like myself are
  faced with the problem of trying to build up a reconcilia-

tion between the two approaches. Some may think it
necessary to more or less undo much that has been learned
in three years of study in the space of one. This means
starting afresh with a view of society which is often presented in unequivocably individualist terms both by the
literature and by the teaching staff on social work courses.
Comparisons /between sociological and social work ideas/
throw up differences of approach which are fundamental
and lead to totally different explanations of behaviour.
It is differences such as these which cause confusion for
many student social workers versed in the sociological
approach.

Role playing appears to be a relatively powerful mechanism of socialisation for the social work student because the
practice roles that are enacted brings the student into close
touch with the realities of the working situation and involve
students in activities which are central and important to the
profession. There is little doubt about the importance of
practical work and of field teaching for the student. In an
unpublished study of former social work students at Leicester
and Oxford Universities, fieldwork teaching was ranked as
the most important element in the training programme
(Stevenson, 1976); as the latter comments 'generations of
students have looked to such field teaching for a most significant contribution to their education and have felt bitterly
disappointed if it did not come up to expectation.' While
there are features of the work situation from which the student is almost too unprotected, there is evidence that the
student may be insulated from some of the organisational
settings of social work (such as the local authority), both
because of the social distance between such organisations
and some social work teachers, and because of the critical
attitude of certain of the latter.

As in other occupations, social work faces the problem of
what it is that practitioners are supposed to be doing and
thus of what is to be taught to students. There appears to
be considerable conflict over the core act in social work
and a great deal of fluidity and change in definitions of this
act which confront the student with choices of the most difficult kind, and which must pose great problems both for students and their progress through the socialising programme
and for those who are themselves responsible for this programme. In the next chapter, some of the solutions adopted
by students to such problems will emerge.

(3) ROLE MODELS

Any process by which a new role is learnt involves something more than the exposure of the newcomer to new situations related to the role; there will also be the necessity
for the newcomer to obtain some idea of the norms of behaviour that attach to the new role. Thus, when an entirely
new role is adopted the newcomer will begin the search for
individuals who exemplify such norms. As Merton et al.
(1957) put it:

> Students, as they begin to learn and practise the profes-
> sional role, often choose a figure in the profession, a
> practitioner known personally or one known only by
> repute, as a model to imitate and an ideal with which to
> compare their own performance. In short they adopt a
> role model.

The question 'how do others behave in the role?' is one of
a number of crucial questions trainees in any profession
ask. The answer, in many cases, is at hand, for the
presence in most socialising programmes of those individuals who hold the new status and play the new role provide
opportunities for newcomers to study this behaviour.
These figures include not only staff involved directly in the
socialising programme but other practitioners not directly
involved but who are known in various ways to the student.
Senior trainees may also be taken as models, providing the
socialising programme gives opportunities for interaction
between different cohorts of trainees and for the development of a student culture based on this interaction.

It is also important to remember that the acquisition of
role models occurs over time and is a continuous process.
Individuals may from an early age be in contact with, or
know about, figures which both serve to shape occupational
choice and provide models for practice. In the case of
medicine and law there is evidence that sizeable proportions
of entrants to professional schools can already name role
models, 68 per cent in the case of medicine and 43 per cent
in the case of law (Merton et al., 1957), a difference which
partly reflects medical students' earlier decisions to enter
professional training compared to law students'. One
implication of a relatively low degree of role model acquisition before entry to professional training is that greater
emphasis is placed on potential role models during the
formal training or socialisation process.

There are a number of dimensions or properties which

attach to role models, and which will influence the outcome
of the socialisation process, including the number of potential models and the extent to which students choose one or
several of these and the degree of identification with a
model.   Models may be close to the student's interests and
future career or distant from them and from the student's
daily activities, and will vary in the extent to which they
establish social distance between themselves and students.
Thus, at one extreme there tends to be a total identification
with a limited number of models who represent similar professional values, are close to the trainees daily activities
and interests and who maintain a minimum of social distance.
This situation is likely to lead on to the acquisition of a
shared and strong sense of professional identity.   At the
other extreme identification with models may be partial and
selective, models may represent differing professional
styles, remain remote from trainees daily activities and
maintain social distance.   This is likely to turn out individuals holding diverse professional values and showing
ambivalence and confusion in professional identities and
career orientation (Bucher, 1969).

The adoption of models by students is therefore a complex
process; Bucher and Stelling's (1977) students were often
vague in their replies to questions about role models and
resisted being pinned down on the subject.   Social work
students on the research course, when asked similar questions, were more certain about their responses but the
modelling process involved was also a complex one.   In
neither study were simple global models identified, in which
students picked out one model and attempted to incorporate
this entirely into their own professional self-conception.
Instead there was great variability in the choice of role
models, and considerable movement in this over time.   In
particular such models were in many instances pieced
together from a number of different sources to make up 'composite' or 'partial' models.

Close to the beginning of their training two-fifths of the
research students could identify a model of some kind near
the beginning of their training and this proportion had risen
to nearly three-quarters close to the end of training (see
Table 8.1).   (While 88 per cent of tech students identified
a role model at this time, double the percentage at the start
of the course, only 56 per cent of university students did
so.)

Students near the beginning of their training identified in

TABLE 8.1 The identification of role models

	Beginning	End
Number of role models	N=37	N=32
(% identifying models)	44%	73%
Identity of models:		
Tutor	12%	17%
Supervisor/fieldwork		
teacher	6%	44%
Other social workers	50%	9%
Composite	26%	30%
Other trainees	6%	-%

the main social workers they had known or knew prior to
training, particularly those with whom they had worked,
including composite models. There was a primary identification with practice rather than the academic or college
setting. Tutors and supervisors played as yet compara-
tively little part in the orientation of students to their
course. This, as well as the choice of a composite model,
is exemplified by a university student near the beginning of
his training,

it fluctuates between two ideas; one is represented by a
Probation Officer I know in Yorkshire – he was univer-
sally known and respected in the area, a community social
worker who did fantastic preventive work. Secondly, a
picture of an almost clinical psycho-therapist, in the
office all the time. I'm not certain the two ideas are
irreconcilable.

This example has something in common with the 'charismatic'
models cited by Bucher and Stelling, that is models who
inspired awe and enthusiasm in trainees; one of their psychiatric students chose Freud as his model.

But there are also the beginnings of certain more realistic expectations of what the course would provide and of
specific elements within it; the importance of the fieldwork
teacher was emphasised by one group of social work students
entering a university course: 'we hoped to gain especially
from the challenge of the supervisor in confronting us with
what we were doing with a case, and how much we knew of
what was going on in our dealing with it' (Butler, 1968).

Towards the end of their course, students' choice of
models were crystallising around the figures of the fieldwork

teacher. This model was selected by over two-fifths of
students, with composite models (usually of a joint fieldwork
teacher/tutor type) ranking second in importance (see Table
8.1). It is interesting to note that the tutors accounted for
less than a fifth of the models chosen and had scarcely
increased in importance since the beginning of the course.

While the importance of the fieldwork teacher might be
inferred both from the practice oriented nature of social
work training and from what is known of the expectations of
new students, the dominance of this figure in the research
courses is a matter of considerable interest and it is
illuminating to see what students identified in such models
before considering the significance of such a choice. This
form of identification is not one that is confined to social
workers. In one study of teacher training, students at the
start of their course saw their college tutors as the group
from which they expected to learn the most in terms of techniques, methods and a general orientation to teaching
(Gibson, 1978). But this changed during the course, particularly after the initial teaching practice, and students
began to look to serving teachers and heads of schools in
which they were working as the group from whom skills and
standards could be acquired. College tutors were viewed
instead as the assessors of practical teaching and students
developed a 'safety and survival' perspective to enable
them to deal with tutors' expectations, and at the same time
looking to serving teachers for advice on how to control the
classroom and teach children, as well as more generalised
images of the teacher as a professional.

One of the most important elements represented by the
fieldwork teachers was their direct and routine contact with
the work of a social work agency in such matters as case-
load management and the balance between work and other
activities. The following extracts are the views of university students reflecting on their fieldwork teachers:

> calm, placid, not flustered; not unduly worried by failure
> and realises that will meet with failure. Able to be a
> personality outside soical work and not too involved with
> cases – sees clients as somebody with a will of own.

> /h̄as the/ ability to apply theory to practice and to see
> how one's own personality is involved in the process.
> Able to have a heavy caseload but not to make a fuss about
> it.

critical of social work's present aims; really does
worry about injustice and inequality. Broadly politi-
cally active and doesn't separate this from social work.
    While the tutors composed a potentially important refer-
ence group, they were not in the main chosen by students.
In part this reflected their distance from the field of practice, graphically described by a first-year tech.
student who commented: 'I don't tend to think of the tutors
as social workers; I think of them as detached from the
field - as "elevated" social workers'. The
fact that the 'elevation' of such figures gave them considerable control over the recruitment and assessment of students, as well as the content and character of the course,
must also be seen in the light of two additional factors, the
relatively limited development of social work theory and the
role of the fieldwork teacher. A model which is fairly
typical of social work courses (including the two research
courses) is for the tutor to attempt to co-ordinate knowledge
from a variety of sources, but to share in the teaching of
professional skills and knowledge with fieldwork teachers.
Yet the latter are in direct contact with the field and perhaps inevitably come to assume greater importance as direct
models. The dilemma for the tutor is considerable, for a
rather insecure academic base is not compensated by the
alternative of presenting an active practice role model,
however much the tutor keeps in touch with practice. One
survey found that only 25 per cent of social work teachers
continue in some form of practice and many do so on only a
token basis, but most regard such activities as an important
aid in teaching (Brown and Webb, 1973). Clearly tutors
will vary in the extent to which they attempt to present
themselves as models at all and whether this is in fact part
of their strategy as teachers.
    One interpretation of the predominance of models drawn
from practice is that this represents 'apprentice socialisation' in which the norms of current professional practice and
a role which is conservative and traditional are emphasised. This compares to an academic model which may provide an opportunity to think abstractly or theoretically
about practice situations and thus lead to progressive or
innovative definitions of practice, which may be discounted
within the confines of daily involvement with practice
(Marsland, 1969).
    While this view might be disputed by those who would
argue that many innovations have arisen from practice

rather than from the academic setting, an interesting comment on the reliance of the student on practice role models
is that this is based on an individualistic conception of education and supervision. As Parsloe and Stevenson (1978)
comment,

> more than any other form of education ... social work
> education has emphasised the need to provide an indivi-
> dual context for learning ... fieldwork placements are
> arranged on the basis of individual supervision. Group
> tutorial and supervisions are almost always something
> added to individual learning.

One implication is that when the student enters practice far
too much is expected from the relationship between the
trained worker and the team leader compared to the alternative of functioning as a member of a team and of actively
using the resources provided by this kind of group.

The importance of 'joint' or 'composite' models underlines
the idea that, like the majority of Bucher and Stelling's
(1977) respondents, social work students do not on the whole
identify with complete models, but tend to build these for
themselves out of a number of disparate elements. As one
tech student said

> I have picked bits out of several people I would like to
> emulate. Firstly, someone with a tremendous range of
> local knowledge and facilities available to clients.
> Secondly, someone calm, unflappable – copes with prob-
> lems at right time, but also discusses everything and
> has facility for forming relationships.

These kinds of choice emphasise the possibility of alternative routes through the socialisation programme, in particular the idea that the student may progress through this
system making his own active choices within it, or alternatively maintaining a considerable degree of freedom from it,
in which the influence of either other students or figures
entirely external to the socialising situation are of much
greater importance than teachers. The idea of 'independent socialisation' (Marsland, 1969) also expresses
adequately the dilemma of the student who is already playing
fully adult roles in the wider society and for whom a particular socialising programme, particularly that of a profession in which there is conflict and disagreement over the
most basic issues, may only touch his life in a most peripheral or marginal fashion.

(4) CONFLICTS IN THE STUDENT/TEACHER RELATIONSHIP

The normal working relationship between fieldwork teacher and student is for the former to be responsible for co-ordinating the work of the student in the agency, as well as providing an educational resource of teaching and learning for the student. The fieldwork teacher is also responsible for providing an assessment of the student's work which will play an important part in the overall final assessment of the student. Clearly the student may be vulnerable in this respect, and the combination of role model, educator and assessor may involve strains, tensions and even conflicts between potentially incompatible elements. Clearly the form of such tensions will vary in relation to changes in the form and content of social work education. Perhaps the most important type of conflict has related to so-called 'therapeutic supervision'. While this form of conflict may be said to characterise the recent past in social work education, research in the 1970s (Mayer and Rosenblatt, 1975) suggests that it is by no means a matter of history. It is also a useful indication of the generation of conflicts by incompatible role definitions among educators.

One particular difficulty in the case of social work is that rarely, if ever, do students see their teachers in direct contact with clients. This makes it difficult for the student to use the teacher, particularly the fieldwork teacher, as a direct role model for his own practice in terms of the skills of the latter. While in theory the fieldwork teacher is the most important potential role model, from the student's point of view there is considerable difficulty in seeing this potential model in action. For example, in the research courses few students mentioned their perception or appreciation of the actual skills and knowledge of their teachers. One of the most important practical ways in which such skills can be demonstrated are in regular supervisory sessions in which the fieldwork teacher had an opportunity to comment (through such practices as process recording) on the handling of cases by the student. This situation can provide the means for the fieldwork teacher to exhibit his own practice skills (and for the student to observe and if necessary absorb such skills) in relation to the student's handling of cases and the part the student's own personality has played in such processes. Blau and Scott (1962) have defined therapeutic supervision as the supervisor's belief that inappropriate handling of clients by a student reflects deficiencies in the student's personality rather than some other feature of the situation. But one element in the situation is that the teacher has little direct evidence of how the student functions with clients, and may use the knowledge gained about the student in supervisory sessions as an indication of this. The supervisory relationship may take on the characteristic of the client/social worker relationship. This type of relationship might also be particularly attractive to the college teacher who is experiencing a recent transition from the practitioner role. As one social work teacher (Woodcock, 1966) has commented on the transition from practice to social work teaching

in the welter of adjustments to these many new duties and responsibilities, the student–tutor relationship may stand out as the one most nearly equivalent to a client–case-worker relationship and in tutorials the tutor may at least recognise something familiar. It is the regular one to one meeting in which ideas and feelings are expressed and he may sit down 'waiting to see what the student brings' in much the same way as he has recently faced clients.

Yet this form of supervisory relationship also raises a number of problems. If the personality rather than the actual work of the student is the focus of attention as well as a feature in the assessment of the student, then this may set up a number of conflicts in the teacher/student relationship, apart from the likelihood that it is not in all instances the best way to demonstrate the skills of the teacher. For example, the student may resent the attention that is focused on him and see through rationalisations of this on the part of the teacher, for example as 'defences' against learning and the achievement of insight. It is, of course, quite possible for students to welcome this state of affairs; one research student compared tutorials with social work interviews, yet in a favourable light because this enabled him to talk about personal problems to a captive audience on a regular basis.

Apart from this form of active compliance it is interesting to note the kinds of coping mechanisms employed by students in the face of supervisory styles that raised problems for them (Mayer and Rosenblatt, 1975). Apart from confronting the supervisors or seeking some form of redress of grievances from higher up in the organisational hierarchy, an important mechanism employed by students was that of 'spurious compliance', in which only an impression of co-operation with supervision is given. One of the students in the study coped by presenting a wholly fictitious account of herself to a supervisor. The idea of concealing true or real reactions to socialisation behind a front will be pursued in chapter 9, but it is important to note that support for various forms of resistance was found in another potentially important group (and one that can also potentially be available as models), other students. Rosenblatt and Meyer cite evidence of the important role that friendships among students played in such situations. Yet it is also the case that the organising and scheduling of many social work courses allow only limited opportunities for a student culture and peer group to emerge (mainly because of the field-work placement) or for a fuller development of supportive relationships among students, including the use of senior students as role models.

Chapter nine

Development and mastery

(1) INTRODUCTION

Those involved in professional education, as well as analysts of this process, have noted that students seem to pass from a stage of heightened enthusiasm and even commitment at the start of their course into what appears to be an emotional doldrums, when the self-confidence with which the student started the course is replaced by anything from a lack of spontaneity and enthusiasm to a situation of crisis in which the student's professional future seems to be at stake. The decline from what has been described as the 'honeymoon' period (Lacey, 1977) can occur in respect of the course itself, personal performance within it or in a more global sense in terms of the particular profession itself.   Other descriptions have included the decline of idealism (Becker and Geer, 1958) and the growth of uncertainty (Fox, 1957). In spite of this, the majority of students are successful in their courses and eventually become full members of their chosen profession.   This indicates that some form of adaptation has occurred and that students have, in a wide variety of ways, come to terms with the situation in which they have found themselves.   Even though the student may be likened to a stranger in a new culture, in most cases he knows enough about the general rules of getting on in society to be able to adapt to this situation.   Unlike the younger student, who may be going through a transitional stage in life in any case and thus occupy a marginal status, older students may have the greatest problem in making their form of adaptation because they are full, adult members of the wider society.
  These observations indicate that socialisation can be approached not only by looking at a series of discrete

experiences, such as the adoption of role models, but as a process marked out by stages, sequences and turning-points and in which the key process is the attempt at the resolution of the dilemmas and conflicts experienced by students. In what follows in this chapter, there will be an attempt to set down some of these stages and the conflicts which they involved both for social work students and those in other professions. In setting out a model in which these stages can be understood and brought together, it is not the intention to suggest that such a model can account for all the variations in student experiences. What is suggested instead is that a range of strategies exist and is made use of by students in a number of differing ways, and that such strategies can be placed within a sequential framework. However this is expressed, the emphasis will be on the student as an active agent making conscious and critical choices within a given context.

Some students, for example the medical internists studied by Bucher and Stelling (1977), experienced a relatively gradual and even development, with few sudden changes and a weak conception of stages – growth did occur but initially in such a way that students were scarcely aware of it.

The notion of stages has a number of different meanings, some of which have little relevance in social work training. One of these is the idea of structurally marked hurdles, such as examinations or tests, which students have to pass in order to proceed to a further stage. Another would be a particular arrangement of activities so that one particular activity must be accomplished before another is attempted. An alternative is to focus on stages in the student's own progress and development within the training process, which Davis (1968) has described as 'doctrinal conversion'. In this the 'lay' views of the trainee are, over time, exchanged for the 'official' views of the professional. This exchange also involves a number of contingencies, such as occasions which are dramatically and emotionally experienced and which are closely related to professional values ('conversion experiences' – ibid.) and trainees' senses of development and mastery (Bucher and Stelling, 1977).

The actual stages in Davis's model can be reduced without much loss of meaning to four: 'initial innocence', 'recognition of incongruity', 'psyching out' and 'provisional and stable internalisation'. While this model was derived from a particular set of socialising experiences (nursing training) which is very different from social work, Davis also suggests

certain issues and questions which are important in any
socialising setting. This model, with certain amend-
ments, will be used as a guide to the discussion that
follows.

One implication of this model is that it concerns the usage
of the term 'profession' by a number of different groups,
including sociologists. While there is no intention here of
repeating the various arguments engaged in by sociologists
and others as to the nature of a profession, the discussion
will inevitably involve professionals' own use of the term as
it concerns themselves and others (such as trainees) and as
it is invoked in the process of what has been described as
'accomplishing profession'. This involves the identification of traits which professionals believe they share and
attempt to pass on to others (Dingwall, 1977). A noticeable
feature of administrative and professional accounts of what
is happening in training concerns the idea that the trainee
is being asked to adopt 'professional' standards and to come
to think of himself as a 'professional' during the training
process.

This chapter, apart from tracing the student's progress
through the socialising programme, will end with an attempt
to identify differences in the outcomes of socialisation for
students from non-manual (or middle-class) and manual (or
working-class) origins, and for students in the different
settings of a university and a technical college.

(2) INITIAL INNOCENCE

Most of those entering professional training come, in one way
or another, from the lay world and bring with them lay concepts of professions and professional tasks. In the case of
Davis's (1968) study of recruits to nursing training, the
imagery which students brought with them consisted of 'a
strong instrumental emphasis on "doing" alongside a secu-
larised Christian-humanitarian ethic of care, kindness and
love for those that suffer.' For Lacey's (1977) graduate
student teachers, their 'honeymoon' period was experienced
as a time of euphoria and heightened awareness, centring
particularly on the experience of leaving the purely academic
courses of school and university for one involving practical
issues, human relationships and (for some) political commitment.

In the case of social work, too, an almost innocent belief

in doing good – in some cases to particular groups (such as children or old people) and in particular contexts (e.g. giving financial or material aid) – characterised the lay imagery of students in the research courses in the early days of training.   Among those with previous experience of the work of the profession, however, there was already an awareness of the simplicity and naivety of these views and the lack of technical expertise they involved.   As one tech student with previous experience of mental welfare work commented, 'I used to see myself as a kind of "mental nurse" in the community, doing first aid and hoping that clients wouldn't have problems.'   In their statement of expectations of the course, one group of university social work students stressed their desire to obtain professional status, indicating knowledge and skill, as opposed to mere 'do goodery' (Butler, 1968).   But the speed with which initial images change varies.   The nurses in Davis's research clung to their early images well into the first year, despite the incongruity of such images.   Not only do social work students have the advantage of more experience in adult life, such as university education or previous work experience, which may serve to dislodge images from the lay world, but they are also subject to early experiences of the work of the profession which may challenge,in quite a fundamental way, such lay images.   The selection process, as suggested, may function in this way, for not only does it challenge the naive motivations of candidates towards 'doing good' and 'working with people', but it also projects the kind of experiences to which students are going to be subjected in training as well as the image of the profession that they will be asked to accept.   Therefore the social work student will begin from an early stage to build up a picture of the situation with which he is confronted and of the possible strategies for survival and success.   The picture of the innocent abroad is thus an exaggerated one.   This is particularly the case for the young recent graduate who has experience of getting through his degree course and of learning the ropes of an institution of higher education.   While the culture presented by social work training may be very different, ground rules for basic survival will have been learnt, including the expectation that the student has the right to successful negotiation of the course in the sense of avoiding failing, even if this means a very low level of demonstrated success in the formal assessment procedure (Davies, 1979a).

(3) RECOGNITION OF INCONGRUITY

As students begin to interact with teaching staff, with other
students (if they are available), and in particular to receive
evaluations of various kinds on their own performance, they
become more aware of the discrepancies between their lay
imagery and that of the profession, represented by the
training institution and its staff.   The point at which such
incongruity is experienced varies with differing socialising
settings, but in the case of the research course social work
students the first experience of supervisory assessments of
practical work and the experience of regular
college-based tutorial sessions were certainly important
turning-points for a number of them.
   These assessments occurred within the first three months
of the course.   The view that 'social work training is not
what we expected' summed up the reactions to the course as
a whole of as many as 70 per cent of the social work students.
Thus students seemed worried about the following kinds of
issues:

   (i)   That instead of concentrating on the real problems,
        personality or situation of those in distress, there
        is instead a focus on the personality of the student,
        his capacities for self-awareness, insight, growth,
        or development.

  (ii)   That the academic part of the course does not always
        appear to be relevant to the development of skills
        which the student needs to develop to help others;
        and that the methods and techniques which it was
        hoped the course would provide are either lacking,
        or are matters over which there is considerable
        dispute.

 (iii)   That the skills and experience of those students who,
        prior to the course, have actually been untrained but
        sometimes experienced practitioners doing the work
        of the profession are being devalued and criticised,
        and they are reduced to the status of newcomers and
        beginners who are treated in the same way as com-
        pletely inexperienced students.   This is similar to
        the process described by Goffman (1961) in his
        account of total institutions and resembles the loss
        of familiar skills described by psychiatric students
        in terms of their previous identities as physicians
        (Bucher and Stelling, 1977).

At this stage most students have only a vague idea of what

they are up against and of the expectations of college and fieldwork teachers; teachers themselves may have only the broadest notion of what they expect from students.   But it is important to try and describe the professional culture which teachers and curriculum represent and the nature of the conflict at this stage between students and their environment.

Wilensky and Lebeaux (1965) have described the situation as a clash between the 'humanitarian' sentiments with which students enter training and the professional and 'clinical' situation which is encountered in training.   The humanitarian seeks to meet needs and problems immediately, accepts the form in which they are expressed, takes people at face value and believes that all men are brothers and should be offered friendship.   The professional clinician, the student is taught, does not view the situation in terms of a naive desire to help, but explores problems with apparent indifference to the client's suffering, does not accept that expressed needs are always real ones, does not accept people at face value and tries to maintain social distance from those he would help.   While many beginning social work students have a greater appreciation of the existence of distinct professional skills than this account would indicate, there is clearly a strongly held belief among students that their motivation to help, and to solve the problems of others, is paramount at this stage.

But by comparison, at the same stage, the teacher's view of the student has been expressed in quite a different way (Hamilton, 1954):

> The student has a naive view of himself as someone who loves and wants to help people and he is full of idealistic and humanitarian feelings.   But he has very little idea of how to help people and counts on classroom teaching and supervision to help him.   In particular if the student is allowed to get away with this he will not be confronted with the many negative and uncomfortable feelings he will have about wanting to help and for which he must be responsible.

A similar view was expressed by a tutor in the research tech:

> Although they /the students/ have expressed an interest in people and are wanting to work with them they have an extra-ordinary lack of interest in wanting to know the real facts or real feelings - they don't know how to look for this ... /therefore/ one has to find ways in the early

stages of shaking them up a bit ... have somehow to be
made aware of their limited perceptions, easy acceptance
of what people say, without being curious about them ...
to look at things intensely and begin to see themselves in
a new light.

The expectations of teachers at this stage, although in
many cases perhaps half understood and partially expressed,
are that the student should be encouraged to shift his self-
image from that of someone who wants to help people to one
who has begun to develop particular skills and techniques of
helping and, through this, has begun to develop a specific
identification with a profession in which these techniques
and skills have been developed and are commonly used.
But the student is also seen as a person who, although
anxious for professional skills, will inevitably have to
experience the negative aspects of confronting deep emotional conflicts in clients (or patients) which will in turn lead to
the arousal of similar emotions in himself (Bucher and
Stelling, 1977).

Such expectations and the clash they represent with the
student's viewpoint present the student with the most serious
problems he is to meet in training, and the manifestations of
this conflict are well recognised features of social work and
other forms of training.　As one former social work student
expressed it, 'I can recall becoming caught up in a flood of
universal doubt in which values, concepts and feelings were
in a complete state of flux' (Keogh, 1968).　The ways in
which the student sees himself are now found to be wanting
in terms of a new, largely unfamiliar environment, and particularly in terms of the definitions of those who have
authority in this environment and who have the power to make
such definitions stick, at least in the eyes of some compara-
tively raw recruits.

The rude awakening of social work students has been doc-
umented by a number of studies.　Shey (1970) concluded
from his study of a representative sample of all American
schools of social work that, 'the overwhelming majority of
American students become disillusioned and highly critical
of the programme [of teaching] shortly after admission to
their respective institutions.'　In a study of adult social
work students in which personality tests were used involving
the measurement of changes in the 'personal constructs' of
students over time, Laycock (1968) found that after four
months of the course students' outlooks were prevalently
'pessimistic' and exaggeratedly self-disparaging ... reflect-

ing a mood of anxiety fairly widespread at that stage of the course.' Psychiatric students also went through a stage of more or less prolonged 'initial anxiety' or 'confusion' lasting from three to ten months (Bucher and Stelling, 1977).

There is an interesting parallel for the student teacher: the enactment of practice roles in the classroom puts a considerable strain on the 'honeymoon' (Lacey, 1977).   One almost panic solution is for the student to attempt to compensate for his inexperience in the classroom by elaborate preparations for lessons and to search for material that will assist in this preparation.   This marks a state of crisis in which many students feel they are not in control of the classroom situation, are failing to get through to the pupils and to teach them anything.   Thus, as Lacey remarks, 'there can be very few professions in which professional induction involves such a high rate of initial failure by the student and rejection by the clients.'

By comparison the social work student, while exposed to the rigours of practice situations from an early stage, is to an extent cushioned from such total exposure to failure in his experiences with clients because of the way in which the student role is defined within the agencies in which the student does his practical work and by the form which his work with clients takes.   This does not mean that the experience with clients is not vivid and real; the evidence of the research courses suggests that students made important decisions about clients and took responsibility for their actions.   This is partly a consequence of the fact that the student is functioning within the agency which exists primarily to provide a service for clients rather than to train students.   Students work with clients of the agency and offer them its services.

Thus social work students had little difficulty (unlike teacher students) in concealing their role as students from their clients.   The main way in which the practitioner role is diluted, and which is clearly a potential contribution to the crisis of the social work student, is that of supervision within the agency.   Most of the research students had at least an hour or more of supervisory sessions in every week of fieldwork practice, which was at the core of the students' learning process.   Supervision consisted mainly of 'process recording' in which students recorded verbatim their interviews with clients.   These were then subjected to analysis and discussion during supervisory sessions. The material which went into process recording is, it is

suggested, analogous to the search for material of the
student teacher at this stage, and the resolution of the
problem brought up by such material is an important indication of the potential for forward movement.   Students
have to make crucial decisions on the form of their interaction with clients and the kind of actions they took as a
result, which may then be subject to critical scrutiny.
This points to an important difference between social work
and teaching; in social work it is likely that the whole
operation of supervision and assessment, and the potential
failure of the student in the short run in these areas, will
make up the situation of crisis or recognition of incongruity
rather than failure or potential failure in the face-to-face
contact with the client, which is likely to characterise
crisis for the student teacher.

   Several avenues are available to students who experience
such misalignment between their own expectations and the
expectations others have of them and who wish to reduce the
dissonance of this situation.   The most obvious is to drop
out of the course at this stage.   In the case of social work
this is very difficult: for example, for students who are
seconded on full pay by their employers to withdraw at this
stage means putting their careers at risk.   For this and
other reasons few students drop out of social work courses
and therefore other means of accommodation and adjustment
are sought.   This suggests a third stage in which there are
attempts to seek out specific solutions to the dilemmas
facing trainees.

(4) PSYCHING OUT: THE SEARCH FOR SOLUTIONS

By this stage in the course it is apparent to most students
that the situation facing them, which has resulted from a
challenge to their lay images of the profession, is unten-
able.   Yet students have to learn to get by in order to
survive in the immediate situation in which they find themselves.   One way in which students may collectively adapt
to this position is to confront staff as to their expectations
and to decide how best to go about satisfying such expectations.   This can be termed 'psyching out' (Davis, 1968).
Staff can be psyched out in a number of ways, ranging from
direct questioning to observation of everyday reactions to
student performances.   One problem is the degree to which
teaching staff are actually able or willing to specify what

their expectations are, or where there are clashes in staff
expectations. This is well expressed by a social work
student (Nyman, 1968) looking back at her first year of
training:

> We spent hours comparing notes, seeking for some en-
> lightenment as to what 'they' wanted. We tried in vain to
> find a common factor between the tutorials given by dif-
> ferent tutors ... after seeking for the significance of
> some of her remarks, hunting for double meanings and
> trying to work out some pattern from our times together,
> I finally burst out in exasperation at my tutor, 'What are
> you looking for?' to be floored by the reply, 'Why should
> I be looking for anything?'

In fact this reply appears less than honest in that there was
little doubt that staff in the research courses did have
expectations of the students, over which there was a fair
measure of agreement. One specific ground rule for survival that was discovered by the research students was that
'fieldwork is of greater significance than academic work' in
the total scheme of the course and in the assessment process. This also approximated to a tech tutor's view of the
situation:

> When it comes to the crunch they [the students] have got
> to get through the exam if only to scrape through; but
> however much they have annoyed college staff, if the
> casework supervisors have felt they are good with
> clients, they are through.

From the kinds of performances students on the research
courses stated they were beginning to enact at later stages
in the course it appeared that psyching out had, in fact,
revealed a particular conception of the professional role,
held by both tutors and supervisors. Students were being
encouraged to take what has been described elsewhere
(Davis, 1968) as a 'psycho-therapeutically objective' view
of the client, that is to appreciate not only what clients say
and do but what they feel, and to subject their own performances to the same kind of theoretical rationale and critique
as that applied to clients. Students were encouraged to
look at their own feelings and attitudes to particular clients
and situations, and to relate their performances (successful
or otherwise) with different clients to elements in their own
personalities.

This marks the beginning of a convergence between student and teacher conceptions of the professional role and is,
for the student, a momentous break with the past. Two

categories of statements seem useful in describing this
change (although they overlap in various ways), those
expressing a sense of development or of having gone through
stages of development, and those expressing a sense of
mastery of necessary skills and knowledge (Bucher and
Stelling, 1977). Such expressions will vary with different
settings and programmes; the psychiatry students in Bucher
and Stelling's study reported a much greater reality to their
feelings of development and mastery than the medical students, for whom such experiences (although vivid) were
seen as part of a smoother progression. Development can
be expressed in terms of changes in relation to other
figures who are significant in training, particularly teachers
but also other students, as well as in the student himself;
mastery can be expressed as a greater general grasp of
important skills, or more specifically where an event was
dramatically experienced in an acute or emergency situation. Medical students referred to the experience of coping
with their first cardiac arrest or renal collapse, psychiatrists of dealing with emergencies, such as patients losing
control in front of them.

These statements of development and mastery were frequently expressed by research course students looking back
on crucial experiences during the course, which involved
both a specific mastery statement and experiences of a
general development in skill and knowledge, such as a
greater capacity to help clients, to work autonomously or to
apply theory to practice. The following are comments made
by a second year tech student and a research university
student (second interview) respectively:

Four interviews ago I sat and watched a woman cry;
before that I would have put my arms around her, now I
don't. It's a detached reasoning process, before it was
all emotional. I can separate out the fact that I am there
to help and not to gratify my own emotions.

I understood what professional work is all about; of what
is going on in the client and myself at the same time.
Made me face up to the relationship between me and the
client.

This kind of statement also indicates models of development held by students, ideas about what they and other students were like at different times. Thus a psychiatry student commented (Bucher and Stelling, 1977):

I can sit with anxious people and not get anxious myself

fairly often.   Now a first year student can't do that,
most of them, for very long.   I can tolerate more
ambiguity, I think, than a first year student – than I
could as a first year student.

Other features of mastery and development are the growth
of personal styles within a more general context of growing
confidence, and the ability to ask for help and to declare a
lack of knowledge.   Here there is a sense that the students
have settled for the course in the sense that they have
moved out of a phase of doubt, difficulty and sometimes open
confrontation with the course and those who run it into an
attitude of accepting an opportunity for learning which by
now has been tested and evaluated (Michael, 1976).

But the idea of settling for the course has also been interpreted as surrender – a surrender of dignity and capacity
for a critical reflection on the meaning of training in
political terms, that is as an incorporation into the bureaucratic machinery of welfare (Piven and Cloward, 1976).
The unspoken rules of social work training are that no
questions are asked while the student passes through the
system and is certificated, 'for these students the educational atmosphere is permeated with mistrust.   Instead of
being permitted to reach out to those from whom they can
presumably learn, they shrink back, fearful and cautious
and expose as little of themselves as possible' (ibid.).

It is also important to acknowledge the link between what
is going on within the student and between the student and
his teachers and clients.   In the case of the assumption of
any new role, the actor will face the problem of the lack of
authenticity and legitimacy in his performance, particularly
if he feels he is merely playing at the business of assuming
the new role.   But if their feelings were never relieved the
actor could never assume new roles or become convinced of
the authenticity of his performance;   he would always feel
that he would be caught out by the audience who would see
his performance as a mere front.   But the student increasingly comes to find that he in fact can convince others of
something of which he is himself in doubt – that his performances are authentic – and he begins to apply to his own
performance the favourable responses others adopt to him.
Thus the sense of inauthenticity begins to lessen and the
student actually 'becomes that status which his performance
claims him to be' (Davis, 1968).

In the research courses, an important element in the
experiences identified by students as expressing develop-

ment, mastery or conversion referred to an evaluation of themselves in the eyes of significant others, by tutor or supervisor in college or agency, or by members of other professions with whom they came into working contact. The following are comments made by a tech student (second year) and a university student (first year):

I had a feeling after I had completed the first year, 'I can't be that bad as they haven't thrown me off the course'; I had the feeling all along that tutors said we weren't a bad bunch.

I had been told that I had done a good piece of work – when I went through my report with the supervisor; one of the probationers – I felt I had got through to him in terms of helping him with difficulties about car stealing – he said I had helped him.

But the resolution of such problems, particularly the convergence between student and teacher, may not always occur or will occur only partially. For example, the assumption of a new occupational role may be seen as quite tangential to some other role, such as marital or familial roles. The commitment to the new professional role may in any case be low at the beginning of the course, or may decline during the course because of disappointed expectations, for example the discrepancies between the realities of practice and the educational programme. Thus the role of student may be played out in a tongue-in-cheek fashion.

The student will also react to particular contingencies with which he is faced and will make a series of adjustments to external demands, so that 'the individual turns himself into the kind of person the situation demands' (Becker, 1971). But, as Lacey (1977) points out, this is only one element in the socialisation process and it is necessary to broaden this idea by adapting the concept of 'social strategy'. This implies that individual actors select ideas and actions within the constraints of a particular situation, and different selections are made by the same actor in different situations. The individual is therefore in constant dialogue with himself about his present and future mode of action. As people interact within the same setting, they can acquire a common mode of acting, or a common strategy, in this case represented by 'student culture'.

The two forms of adjustment so far described by social work students are well illustrated by Lacey's types of social strategy, internalised adjustment and situational compliance.

In the latter, the individual complies with the constraints of
the situation, and of authority figures within it, but retains
private reservations about them in the form of the front
and of instrumentalism.   He is merely seen
to be good.   In the former, the individual complies with the
constraints and believes that these are for the best.   He
really is good, and actually believes in the kind of socialising experiences in which he is involved as a real shift
towards a legitimately desired object.

One feature of the situation in which the research university students were placed deserves particular mention, that
is the existence of a T-group at which attendance was voluntary (although the majority of students attended) and which
was run by a group worker not on the staff of the college.
This group and the experiences students reported within it
seemed to have considerable importance at a crucial mid-
point in the course when change was in the air.   For some
the group had a most dramatic effect.   According to one
university student:

the T-group crystallised the whole situation, was 'the
compression of the compression', the nub on which the
whole course swung ... aware that /in the T-group/ we
were being put in a situation of extreme anxiety ... value
of this that in reacting to stress situations it teaches you
lessons.

The use of such groups in social work training has the
dual function of providing a knowledge of group dynamics
and group work, and of increasing self-awareness, but it is
this very duality which has led to criticisms of the use of
groups in training.   While some assert that it is possible
to draw a clear line between therapeutic and educational
concerns, a criticism is that this may involve coercing the
individual by therapeutic procedures (Davies, 1973).
Again, although T-group membership on courses is normally
voluntary, the difficulty of this is that students may feel that
failure to participate will affect their final assessment.

While the focus on the self of the student is a feature that
social work training undoubtedly involves (although it is not
unique to this form of education), it was clear from the
research courses that this involvement was felt by some to
be an optional feature that could be taken up as desired and
that students could make a variety of choices - for example,
that while the professional self could be a legitimate object
of attention, the extension of this to other areas of the self
was to be resisted.   As one university student commented

'the social worker must be in touch with the self, but only in relation to work.'

An extreme reaction was the rejection of any involvement of the self; here the therapeutic conception of social work which underlies the principle of involving the self of the student is viewed critically, as by this university student (second interview):

Tutorials haven't been academic; you must be emotionally involved with the course, an emotional catharsis. There is a pressure to talk about own problems – have been resisting this, not my way of thinking about social work. Casework is done on you: but do they /the tutors and supervisors/ put you in a client situation to further your ability to do the job?

Reactions of this kind were also associated with a rejection of T-group membership. Thus responses to the pressure of self-involvement varied along an acceptance-rejection continuum. Certainly by the end of the course a small group of students could be identified (more numerous in the university than the tech) who constituted a deviant minority in the sense that they rejected some of the values and practices (including that of self-involvement) on which the courses were based.

These reactions also call into question the distinction made in training between the professional self, which is held to be a legitimate object of attention during training, and other aspects of the self on which attention is not focused. The types of reaction noted above suggest that this is a difficult distinction for students to make, even in cases where the rationale for the distinction was accepted. In other cases, the heightening of self-awareness in the professional sphere, and the extension of this to the private sphere, appeared to be accepted and even welcomed.

However, another interpretation of the emphasis on small groups (including T-groups) in training is that they provide an alternative focus to dyadic or one-to-one groups and lessen the strains inherent in the latter. Although dyadic relationships are clearly an important way of focusing on the self of the trainee they also make considerable demands on the participants, primarily because they are dependent upon the participation of both members, so that the group is threatened by the withdrawal of one member. Dyads also foster both a sense of closeness and intimacy and a constraining sense of interdependence. The dyadic relationship, combining elements of closeness, intimacy and con-

straint, may be characterised almost as an act of faith
(Glasner, 1977).

However, if the dyad becomes extended to include three
or more members the individual will feel less demand upon
him, since the withdrawal of any one member does not
threaten the group as such. Another feature of the dyad is
that while some areas of the self are focused upon, others
may be closed off (Rustin, 1971). In the triad, the individual will have to face many more possibilities for self-
expression and self-analysis, but may be freed for this
purpose because of the less stringent demands made upon
him by the group. Another effect of third-party membership is mediation between the other two members, thus
integrating potentially disruptive relationships.

The theory of triadic relationships also has implications
for the socialisation process itself (ibid.). In groups of
more than two persons the self of the individual is confronted not only by a variety of different dyadic relationships
but also by the cognitive equivalent of such relationships,
that is the existence of a plurality of viewpoints, attitudes,
and beliefs.

Thus triadic, or small group, relationships, function not
only to open up areas of the self left untouched or defended
in dyads, but may open up a range of beliefs and attitudes,
and dislodge the idea of truth as residing in conformity to
one self-evident doctrine.

(5) INTERNALISATION

Despite the fact that the dramatic events of the previous
stage are, for most students, not to be repeated, the final
stage prior to the termination of the course is not uneventful, being concerned with both final assessment and the
emergence of the student into the working world as a new
but inexperienced member of a professional community, with
all the anxieties that inevitably surround this. However,
the student is supported in this transition by the likelihood
of a successful assessment of his competence which acts as
a public recognition of a growing sense of mastery and professional development. This has been described in terms
of 'provisional' and 'stable' internalisation (Davis, 1968),
the former characterised by a tendency for students to
retain a 'subterranean' attachment to their previously held
lay imagery and a reawakening of feelings of doubt about

career choice, motivation and suitability for the work, as
well as doubt about newly acquired skills. In social work
training this is sometimes exacerbated by a structural
feature of training, a long practical placement lasting well
beyond the official academic term in which academic
teachers may have less impact and in which the student may
feel over-exposed. At the other end of the spectrum are
those who have (to them) achieved final mastery – as one of
Bucher and Stelling's medical students commented: 'Right
now I can handle any problems in internal medicine that any
board certified can handle.' A number of phenomena seem
to characterise a movement towards a more stable internalisation, particularly an increasing closeness and identity
with professional rather than student culture, including the
emergence of positive and negative reference models and the
use of professional rhetoric.

The movement towards professional culture was shown on
the research courses by the acceptance of the definitions of
social work that were dominant in those courses at the time.
Thus 9 out of 10 students on the research courses at this
stage had an image of social work in which understanding of
clients' feelings and emotions were either of greatest importance in practice or were of equal importance to the provision of material aid. The early lay image of a generalised
helping relationship in which material aid played an important part had almost completely disappeared. The students
in Laycock's (1968) study had, near the end of their course,
also reversed their early tendency to self-disparagement
and their attitudes had changed in a direction consistent
with the attitudes then expected of social workers.

Professional training is marked by the use of technical
vocabularies which function not only as a technical language
which fosters communication, but also as a means by which
the student can delineate a particular field of work and come
to see himself as a professional as distinct from a layman.
In nursing training there are a number of technical terms in
use which perform this function, such as 'patient needs' or
'responsibility' (McGuire, 1966) which students come to
understand and use. Particular sub-cultural settings
therefore generate their own language, and in social work
training terms such as 'capacity for growth', 'movement',
'insight' and 'self awareness' are examples of approved
rhetoric which seem to perform much the same function.
The use of professional rhetoric (or theory) helps to re-
assure the students that they are now different persons,
that is 'professionals'.

A university student near the end of his course makes this point:

Client on probation: her mother started to talk about her in the same terms as we had been using in the office. Their family situation had been a very typical one, and a 'crisis' had been identified – reassured me about the value of theory.

Similarly, those who come to use professional rhetoric (both staff and trainees) may be defined as positive role models with which to identify as against the negative role models also encountered in practice who exemplify 'bad practice'.

Apart from negative role models in the profession into which the trainee is entering, such as the untrained practitioner or the student who fails assessment (however sympathetically this is viewed at the time), an important source of negative models are other professionals with whom work is normally shared and who may also be important sources of power and resources in the professional network.

While 'atrocity stories' are told by clients about professionals, they are also important in any situation where 'outsiders' (such as students) seek to become recognised as competent members of a group, where such stories are part of the repertoire of that group (Dingwall, 1977). Such negative models are important for students because they are something that can be shared with established professionals, particularly where such stories are part of the folklore of the profession. In the case of the health visitors, there is often a portrayal of the professional as a heroic figure who triumphs over the incompetence of others (particularly general practitioners), or who maintains a personal, professionally 'correct' version of what inter-professional relations should be (ibid.). This involves an active and protective role in relation to professional culture and knowledge and an assertion that outsiders (the untrained and other professionals), are therefore incompetent – for example a senior nursing student openly challenged doctor's orders on a hospital ward round on the basis of nursing research (Simpson, 1967).

Among the negative models which are found within the same profession are certain of the student's own teachers, who are gradually losing their immediate power over the student – the latter is moving on to assume a new role while the teacher remains in the same position, possibly even feeling the necessity for a defence and reinstatement of the

teacher role. Atrocity stories are also relevant here,
where teachers cling to out-of-date theories, are long
distant from the field of practice, or are seen as being in
possession of inappropriate values, such as aloofness from
students or very dated concepts of staff/student relations.
At the least, students might well require a redefinition of
roles in relation to teaching staff, exemplified by an attempt
in one course review to give staff explicit advice about
issues such as the restructuring of course material and the
style of staff/student relations (Michael, 1976). Thus the
merging of student and staff cultures is not a total or uncritical process – rather a dialogue between groups at different career stages and with rapidly diverging interests.
    The idea of the student as 'worker' certainly dominated
the end of the course studied by Michael and seemed to constitute a major form of resolution for teachers. As one
teacher commented, 'It has happened earlier this year,'
indicating a transition between the student who had settled
for a course of studies and someone who was almost a professional colleague and worker and who also was able to
evaluate and share some of the basic principles of the educational process in social work. It is also important to
remember that the student's new identity has been created
largely in the sheltered world of college or as a student
member of a social work agency, and this somewhat fragile
professional self may well come under pressure in the
normal working environment.

(6) OCCUPATIONAL IDENTIFICATION

In the account presented so far in this chapter we have
examined the picture of the student as someone who is
experiencing social work training as a process of development and mastery, one who is concerned in particular with
a series of stages of development. This largely ignored
the specific outcomes of socialisation, and the possibility of
differences in outcome in different educational settings.
One intention of the original research by the author was in
fact to compare social work education in a university and a
technical college course. In this final section a number of
aspects of occupational identification are drawn together in
terms both of student class origins and the two different
college settings, material which is derived entirely from the
original research in the absence of other research in this
area.

There was very little indication from this research that the class background of students had made much difference to the outcome of the socialisation process. For example, rather similar proportions of students with manual and non-manual backgrounds had an image of themselves as 'social workers rather than students' by the end of the course, were members of a social work professional association, or had identified a role model. One suggestion from previous research was that the 'marginal' student (whose biographical roots are in one social world but who is currently operating in another and different world) will make a particular form of occupational adjustment characterised by a high level of identification with an occupation, its values and institutions (Varley, 1968; Box and Ford, 1967; Cotgrove and Box, 1970). In this way, the strains experienced by the socially or occupationally mobile are reduced by a total immersion in the new occupational environment which makes it easier to break with an existing background, or at least makes the latter less visible. Although no test of values was carried out in the research which is being reported here, there is little evidence on the criteria that were used that students with manual, working-class backgrounds made this kind of extreme form of occupational identification as a solution to the problem of marginality. It is also the case that students with such backgrounds have not identified any less with the culture represented by social work training than have those with non-manual backgrounds.

When the differences relating to college setting are considered, the similarities rather than the differences in identification are also evident. Similar proportions (88 and 94 per cent) of both university and tech students had a 'social work self-image', were members of a social work professional association (37 and 38 per cent) or thought that membership was important (86 and 94 per cent). The main differences between university and tech students lay in attitudes to social work as a profession. Much smaller proportions of university than tech students believed either that social work had obtained professional status (19 compared to 56 per cent), or that it was important that professional status be sought (68 compared to 100 per cent). This reflected a rather more critical and reflective stance on the part of the university students towards social work at this point in time. But the outcome of the socialisation process noted here casts doubt on some of the criticisms of the extension of social work training to non-university institutions, particularly that this would result in a less than satisfactory identification with the social work profession compared to university training. The evidence here is that the non-university courses may be no less effective in this respect than other longer-established courses.

Chapter ten

Assessment

(1) INTRODUCTION

Apart from the selection and organisation of knowledge into curricula, students are also assessed on their understanding of this knowledge and, in professional training courses, on their capacities for the application of knowledge in practice. Assessment procedures are therefore an aspect of the social organisation of knowledge, although one that has until recently been given relatively little attention either by sociologists or professional educators. Yet partly as a result of criticisms of the professions from a variety of sources, professional educators (including social workers) are now looking with a more critical eye at the whole process of assessment and evaluation.

One of the functions of any professional training school or course is the assessment of competence to practise, and the exclusion from the ranks of qualified practitioners of those judged to be non-competent. This process relates not only to the occupation itself, its identity and search for professional status, but to the continuing renewal of the 'contract' between the occupation and the wider society for the delivery of minimum standards of practice. In a sense, professions owe their status and rewards to the establishment of such a contract, to the effect that certain standards of competence will be maintained. Autonomy as well as status and rewards are the major consequence of the establishment of this contract. Assessment procedures represent the renewal of such a contract which can also be likened to the defence of the public interest, implying the protection of the potential client public from those deemed as unfit to practise. The term 'assessment procedures' can, therefore, be described

(Dingwall, 1977) as the search by the examiners for information about the candidates which would allow them to
justify the grant of a licence to practise as a qualified
practitioner (although in some professions, including social
work, those who are unqualified are also able to practise).
This search for information can also be described as the
sanction which in fact underpins the form of social order
which a training course represents.

Just how far professions are able or even attempt to
adhere to this theoretical model have been matters of specu-
lation. The 'search for information', for example, depends
upon such factors as the availability of information and
agreement between different parties to the assessment procedure on what constitutes relevant information which has to
be taken into account. For example, in some training programmes the 'actuarial' principle of grading and assessment
of students along traditional academic lines plays little part
in the assessment of either academic work or fieldwork.
Instead of fine distinctions between grades or marks, the
main principle of assessment is 'contractual', representing
an interpretation of the student's progress in the course
drawn particularly from written reports by teachers and by
the students themselves (Dingwall, 1977). A somewhat
similar distinction has been made between the assessment
'event', a system of testing involving a judgment and a decision about the suitability of a student for the award of a
qualification, and the assessment 'process' in which a
student's development over time, his strength and weaknesses, may be reviewed in a joint exercise which is partly
for the benefit of the student and where feedback may be
obtained (Brandon and Davies, 1979).

Again, attitudes to the assessment process may vary considerably between the different groups involved. In
Morrell's (1979a) account of the assessment process in
social work, different parties to the proceedings justified
assessment in rather different ways. College tutors
adhered to the idea of assessment as a renewal of the profession's contract to safeguard standards for the sake of the
client public, and gave only secondary consideration to the
importance of the achievement of learning objectives or the
progress of students. But other groups (fieldwork teachers,
other agency staff and students) were agreed in justifying
assessment primarily in educational terms as indicating
strength and weaknesses and facilitating further progress.
Students in particular believed that the assessment process
was primarily a way of helping them through the course.

But even among teachers within a profession, attitudes to assessment may differ in other ways – for example in terms of segmental affiliations.   Those in different segments may look for different indications and utilise different criteria in assessing students just as they did in their initial selection.   These kinds of differences may be embedded in a more general atmosphere of changes in the way educational systems operate.   For example there has been a trend away from the use of the unseen formal examination as the primary tool of assessment towards the use of a mixture of examination and other forms (such as essays and projects), a change which has also been evident in social work education (Hayward, 1979).   At one extreme are those professional groups who deny the validity of assessment or feel that assessment, for one reason or another, is an almost impossible task. Probably more typical of those who have the greatest   difficulty with assessment are teachers who give the vaguest of possible reasons for student failure;   this accounted for a fifth of the respondents in Morrell's 1979 study.

Apart from the means by which teachers attempt to get information about students for assessment purposes, whether by examination, coursework or from reports on students' progress, students will also attempt to obtain knowledge about their progress by seeking indications, or 'cues', relating to this both from others and from themselves – the latter can be described as 'self-generated' cues (Bucher and Stelling, 1977) or 'self-evaluation'.   In chapter 9 an indication was given of the importance of validation in the eyes of others as a form of resolution of the problem faced by students in making their way through the course. Clearly cues from others will be important, either in terms of formal assessments at particular points in the course (such as mid-course supervisors' reports, essay and examination grades, as well as final assessment) or of more informal indications at other points in time on a more random basis.   Interestingly, neither formal written evaluations to which students had access nor grades were of overriding importance for many of Bucher and Stelling's respondents – they relied more on direct cues in terms of what they were told, or indirect cues inferred from the behaviour of teachers – for example, if teachers or senior students seemed to be treating them more like colleagues than before.

But self-generated cues are also important, and a student will evaluate himself on the basis of the success or failure of the work that he has done. Such cues were for Bucher and Stelling's respondents more important than cues from others. These cues are even encouraged by certain assessment schemes where self-evaluation is encouraged and where students participate with their teachers in the assessment process. An important feature of self-generated cues, which will be highly relevant to the discussion in the final chapter, is the 'discounting' of cues, that is, the rejection by students of cues which they defined as irrelevant or as coming from a source that was seen as unimportant or discredited.

(2) THE STRUCTURE OF ASSESSMENT: ACADEMIC ASSESSMENT

In social work, like other practising professions, assessment is comprised of a balance between academic, college-based work and practical fieldwork, in which the latter makes up about half the time spent by the student in his course. Students are required to pass in both elements and no compensation is allowed between academic and fieldwork assessments. They can therefore be treated to some extent separately (and have been so treated in the literature), although an organising principle in social work education is that of the 'integration of theoretical knowledge with practice', and the attempt is made to assess students on their ability to put knowledge into practice. Yet the difficulties of this principle are considerable, not the least of which is that those responsible for the assessment of students' fieldwork abilities are practising social workers who work in agencies distinct from the college setting, although the final responsibility for the assessment of the student is in the hands of college teachers and college boards of examiners, on which field teachers are not normally represented or are accountable (Brandon and Davies, 1979). This is but one example of the tenuous relationship between academic and fieldwork assessments although there are a number of examples of attempts to bridge this gap through panels of college and fieldwork teachers and numerous variations in the relationship between college and agency (see Michael, 1976, for a detailed study of one example).

Academic assessment is organised mainly as either a mixture of formal examinations and other methods (such as essays or projects) or as a mixture which excluded examina-

tions. In Hayward's (1979) study of a sample of social
work courses the former method predominated (on only one
course was assessment by examination only). In the
research courses, the tech.assessment system was an
example of the former method and the university system of
the latter. It is interesting to note the reactions of the
university students to this new and then rather unfamiliar
method, which was a sharp break with their undergraduate
experiences. The main impact of the new methods was their
focus on the 'self' of the student and on 'whole person learning' - processes which could not be assessed by examination 'The self was not touched by knowledge before this
course - I was just a minor member of a large year' (university student, second interview); 'Self not really involved
in a theoretical course - this course gets at you' (university
student, second interview).

In reality, for both sets of students the experience of
assessment was new, for while many of the tech students
had the familiar experience of examinations to deal with, the
experience of other forms of assessment, particularly
academic and fieldwork teachers' reports, was a new one as
well. In particular, the experience of evaluation at times
other than formal assessment (described variously as 'continuous assessment' or 'evaluative assessment' - Hayward,
1979) where in both college and fieldwork settings there was
the possibility that everything students said and did could
be 'taken down and used in evidence', produced a sense of
pressure as great as and certainly very different from the
more traditional system. This was especially the case for
graduate students who had become used to a more relaxed
regime. As one graduate student put it, 'you felt that can't
lapse at all - that missing one lecture would have cost me my
diploma.' Other problems included the difficulty some students had in assessing themselves and of discussing this
with the supervisor.

Perhaps of greatest importance was the new and more
complex network of relationships between students and staff
which this system produced. In more traditional situations
external examinations unite student and teacher in the task
of getting the better of the examiner; this results in a relatively simple and fairly conflictless relationship (Taylor,
1969). Even in cases where the role of teacher and
examiner is combined the situation is not much complicated
because there will be an assumption of objectivity in the
marking of exams on the basis of standards which are

largely outside the staff/student relationship. Students
can only play a part in this by attempting to spot questions.
But continuous assessment greatly complicates the situation
in which staff and students find themselves and considerably
increases the problem of objectivity in assessment. Thus
Shipman (1966) showed in his study of a teacher training
college that final decisions on students with poor examination results were always made on the basis of tutors' views
of the characteristics of students and never on results
alone. Again, if staff have many opportunities for face-to-
face contact with students, and this is combined with continuous assessment, this provides considerable opportunity
for tutors to influence a student's academic and personal
development and for students to exert pressures of various
kinds upon tutors.

(3) FIELDWORK ASSESSMENT

The structure of fieldwork assessment is aimed formally at
identifying minimum standards of competence which will
justify the award of the Certificate of Qualification in Social
Work (the CQSW). The main evidence available to the
assessors is based primarily upon reports from fieldwork
teachers who will usually indicate whether the work of the
student is or is not up to a particular standard of competence. At the same time, responsibility for arriving at
this decision may also lie between the fieldwork and
academic teacher or teachers – although it seems likely
that increasingly the fieldwork teacher is now normally
expected to take the responsibility for recommending an
appropriate grade (Brandon and Davies, 1979). While it is
the board of examiners, of which the academic teachers are
members, who will make the final decision, there does
appear doubt about who has the final responsibility for
recommending a decision; 'the responsibility for saying that
a student should fail bobs about between a variety of people,
some of whom are less than happy about accepting it'
(Morrell, 1979b).
    The evidence of a student's practice competence is
obtained by reference to what a student says he has done or
what he has written (for example in terms of process
recording), self-evaluation and a description of the work
that has been done in the placements. Because of problems
such as confidentiality, the student is rarely observed

directly by his teachers in his work with clients which
means that reliance has to be placed partly on impressions
gained at a distance: 'during apprenticeship in social work
one is rarely observed by seniors at the coalface ... and
the supervisor has to rely on impressions gained at secondhand' (Sparrow, 1978). Such impressions can be based on
evidence obtained from regular supervisory sessions
between fieldwork teachers and students, or from meetings
between these two and tutors or between students and tutors.
Morrell (1979b) has quantified the time taken on these meetings to a weekly average of eighty, ten and fourteen minutes
per week respectively. But evidence may be of a more
direct kind, for example, where an oral examination is given
based upon a brief account of a piece of work that has been
done as well as teachers' reports. Here it is performance
in the oral rather than teachers' recommendations that make
up a successful fieldwork assessment (Parsloe and Stevenson, 1979), whilst the oral examination meant a heightened
sense of anxiety, this seems to have brought the best out of
students individually, and through mutual support. Another
indication of a student's work is the preparation of a port-
folio of work a student has done on the placement which may
also be available to examiners. Experiments are also
being made with more direct evidence of a student's practice, such as audio and video recordings or the direct
observation by fieldwork teachers of a student's performance. The limitation on the use of such procedures is
partly the need to protect the rights and privacy of clients
and the confidentiality of the proceedings, as well as the
fact that the intrusion of technical equipment and third
parties alters the nature of the one-to-one situation between
social worker and client.

Apart from the mechanics of the fieldwork assessment
process, and associated problems such as variation in the
skill and experience of fieldwork teachers and the previous
experience of students, the fundamental issue is the fact
that attempts to set down minimum standards of practice are
inevitably related to the wider problem of defining the nature
of the professional task in social work, and thus of the basis
for assessment. Numerous attempts have been made to do
this in official accounts (see for example BASW, 1977;
CCETSW, 1975), but these seem to have the common characteristic of being phrased in very general terms which leave
to courses the tasks of clarifying the skills involved in
basic competence (Brandon and Davies, 1979). One way of

approaching the problem of an understanding of what does
actually happen in practice, and thus of what minimum
standards are in fact applied, is by looking at the nature of
student failure in social work courses, that is of attempting
to generalise from those students who might be defined as
marginal when the decision to award or withhold professional certification is made.

(4) THE LIMITS OF COMPETENCE

Student failure is rare in social work training and one of
the reasons for this is the attempt that is made to exclude
those students who may be at risk from entering courses
through a rigorous selection process.   From this it might
be inferred that the contract that professional training
involves, in which the individual who is considered unsuitable for practice is not awarded a certificate of qualification, has been fulfilled.   But it has been suggested that as
many as 5–6 per cent of all those actually obtaining the
CQSW are not competent in practice at a minimum level
(Brandon and Davies, 1979).   Brandon and Davies suggest
that one feature of the problem is the tendency for social
work courses to lay stress upon the assessment 'process'
rather than the assessment 'event', that is the final decision made by examination boards as to the competence of the
candidate in the course as a whole.   The evidence on which
this is based is a study of 208 final year students, on 6
courses, in which only 4 students failed to obtain a qualification in social work (the CQSW).   A group of 35 students
who were defined by teaching staff as 'at risk' of failing
was studied.in detail.   Even where there was considerable
evidence of problems occurring in students' fieldwork (see
Table 10.1 for an analysis of the types of problems found)
the tendency was in most cases to give the student the
benefit of the doubt when it came to intermediate and final
assessment.   Even where tutors or fieldwork teachers had
basic doubts about various facets of the student's work,
with very few exceptions, direct evidence which tended to
demonstrate the competence of the student received less
emphasis than evidence which showed lack of actual incompetence.   As the authors comment, 'It was generally
assumed that a pass grade should be given if there was no
evidence of incompetence, rather than positive evidence of
good practice.'   This reflected genuine divisions of opinion

TABLE 10.1 Assessment problems referred to by tutors
(source: J. Brandon and M. Davies, 1979)

	Number of assessments with problems in these areas (N = 35)
Activity with clients and others in the client's environment	28
Attitudes and values expressed in the work	13
Ability to work within the agency	22
Communication through reports, letters, file and process records	24
Availability and application of relevant theory	12
Student as a learner including use of supervision	13
Professional presentation	6
General conduct and behaviour at the placement	9

between teachers, but also confusion as to where the responsibility for final decisions lay and variations in assessment procedures. Other influences external to the assessment procedure — such as the suitability of placements and the short length of training — were also important factors.

One of the most important problems that teachers found students had experienced were activities in relation to clients. This included difficulties students had in developing relationships with clients, in studying their own interaction with clients and even in meeting or visiting clients. To this can be added difficulties students had in presenting themselves as professionals in terms of their colleagues and teams. Another area of difficulty lay in work within the agency, particularly in relating to colleagues and with other agencies including making adequate records and communicating adequately with colleagues in written form.

A number of explanations can be advanced for the tendency for the passing of the marginal student, some of which echo previous points made about the nature of social work education. Division of opinion among the assessors, whether they are academic or fieldwork tutors, are reflections of the segmental nature of social work and of segmental

allegiances.   This reflects in turn the difficulties of
defining the nature of social work and the kinds of tasks for
which students are being prepared.   Assessment in community work appeared to be a particular problem in the
Brandon and Davies study, indicating the identification of
this speciality with the radical segment within social work
in which a much wider range of working styles and looser
definitions of competence seem apparent.   Another conflict
relates to the acceptance in certain areas of higher education, particularly at undergraduate level, that an award
of some kind be made in most cases even to the most marginal student, but that this be signified by a low or pass
grade.   This expectation can inform the attitudes of both
teachers and students and leads to the attempt to reward
the student for such factors as development and attendance
rather than merit, and also avoids applying the labelling
and stigmatising definitions of failure.

(5) CONCLUSION

The twin processes of selection and assessment for any
form of professional training are the basis for the renewal
of the contract between a profession and society.   Any
problems which arise over either process cast doubt upon a
particular profession's capacities to maintain a valid and
reliable mechanism for the socialisation of new members,
and thereby to exercise the control that is necessary over
such members for the granting and renewal of the contract.
The research on the limits of competence which has been
noted in this chapter has attracted much comment and criticism from within social work, not only on the basis of the
generalisation from a small sample of courses and students
to the whole social work student population, but also for
the degree of what is seen as unjustified self-criticism in
time of stress and conflict for social work (Parsloe and
Stevenson, 1979).
     However, such strictures also ignore the fact that pro-
fessional education is typically the subject of extreme conflict, not only between the groups involved but between the
principles inherent in that educational process.   One particular form of conflict which receives less attention than it
should, but which is inherent in the model of professional
socialisation presented here, is that not only are there differences and conflicts between teachers (which are expres-

sed in differences over issues such as assessment), but
that these are also present in the relationship between students and teachers. The idea of these two groups being
united in the pursuit of professional competence or excellence is remote from reality. Conflicts between teachers
may lead to conflicting principles and goals (although these
may be inherent in any educational system), and this provides the possibility of a regulation of this situation by the
student, who is a more active participant in the educational
process than his counterpart in the 1950s or earlier, and
who is encouraged by many educational programmes to take
such a part in his own educational environment. An example
of this is that many social work courses represent an educational environment which emphasises the idea of evaluation and
assessment as partly a joint enterprise, where self-evaluation by the student is encouraged as an aspect of both professional and personal growth which reflects the concern of
teachers with the self-consciousness and personal development of their students. The student is in general encouraged
to become an active agent and this is institutionalised not
only in terms of routine self-evaluation, but by a whole
gamut of situations ranging from course reviews, committees
and meetings up to appeals against decisions by boards of
examiners. At the same time, this means the possibility
that negative cues from teachers may be only too easily discounted, not necessarily as coming from a source which is
discredited, but a source which is one among others, and
not necessarily one that is given the greatest prominence.
Against this is the attempt to achieve another educational
and professional objective, the application and maintenance
of an assessment scheme which commands the minimum
acceptance of all concerned with the teaching and administration of the courses. Clearly there is considerable scope
for conflict between the aims of student involvement in
matters of assessment (as well as in the more general processes relating to the course) and the application of a fairly
consistent assessment scheme at a particular point in time.
Expectations built up during a course on the basis of the
former objectives may seem impossible to realise in terms
of the latter, and teachers may feel in an exceptionally weak
and vulnerable situation as a result. This vulnerability is
also added to by the small scale and isolated nature of a
number of social work courses, and the close personal relations which characterise a system not based upon examination alone. The college teacher is also vulnerable because

he has to perform the difficult job of interpreting field-
workers' reports on students for assessment purposes
written in an entirely different occupational environment
subjected to contingencies with which he cannot be entirely
familiar.   This reflects a situation where academic and
practical training go on in separate and distinct situations.
But the student is also vulnerable and is faced with all the
uncertainties both of professional training and of the practice that is to follow.   One response to this is to take up
the opportunities provided by conflicting educational principles, for the negotiation of a safe passage through a difficult situation.

One response to these difficulties has been an attempt to
arrive at a series of agreed assessment procedures on the
part of CCETSW (1980b).   This involves the specification
of a minimum length of assessed placement together with
broad areas of social work knowledge and specific skills to
carry out a variety of tasks in practice situations on which
students will be assessed.   The latter includes the establishment of relationships with individuals and groups,
advocacy, mediation and collaboration with other professions, and the use of skills in interviewing and groupwork.

While these guide lines will command a measure of agreement among social workers (they have been supported by
BASW) they will also raise again the conflict between administrative and academic interests.   While there is no intention on the part of CCETSW of suggesting a national curriculum for CQSW courses, the guide lines will be interpreted
by some as increased control over training courses and a
threat to the autonomy of training institutions.

Chapter eleven

Conclusion

(1) THE 'CRISIS' IN SOCIAL WORK EDUCATION

Each year in Britain over 3,500 students successfully complete the courses of training in social work leading to the
basic nationally recognised award of the CQSW, while other
students complete different forms of occupational training in
this area.   These figures mark the growth in social work
education particularly since the 1960s.   At the same time,
social work and social work education is today the subject
of internal and public discussion which has not occurred
since the publication of the Younghusband Report in 1959
and the Seebohm Report in 1968.   In 1980 an official committee of inquiry was appointed to inquire into the definition
of the social work task.   These discussions reflect a
number of factors both outside and inside social work,
including the effect of declining state support for higher
education in a period of economic instability as well as
growing internal debate on a number of issues, ranging from
the appropriate knowledge and skills that social workers
should possess and obtain as a result of training, to the
problems of the assessment of such competence.   One additional feature is the likelihood of a relative or absolute
decline in student numbers as the untrained workers are
trained and resources for further manpower and training
are cut.   Similar controversies have characterised the
recent history of social work elsewhere; thus 'crises' have
been diagnosed in American social work education – in 1970
centring upon falling state support for schools of social
work (Rosen, 1970) and later (Boehm, 1976) surrounding
the differing educational needs of new categories of workers
and the ever-widening fields of social work practice.   A

particular feature of the controversy in British social work today is one that is basic to arguments about professionalism – namely, the question of control over education and training, in particular what is seen by some as the growth of external administrative control over the activities of departments of social work training (including the possibility of a national curriculum) and the appointment to the latter of those in senior academic positions but who are not professionally qualified in social work.

In the case of social work one factor in addressing such issues is the paucity of research in social work education, not only on the structure and content of courses but on the process of socialisation itself. While attempts are being made to fill this gap (particularly recent and forthcoming CCETSW and DHSS studies) evidence about the actual situations in which students and teachers find themselves is overshadowed by assertions and arguments about what the educational process should consist of which resemble almost theological debates. In particular, those involved are themselves deeply embedded in administrative or educational roles, and their words at times appear the only source of information or comment. One response to the contemporary 'crisis' is to ask what implications research within the tradition of sociological and social-psychological studies of professional socialisation can have for the issues under discussion and for those responsible for planning and implementing training programmes, including research which documents the experience of other professions in the training process. This book has attempted to bring together some of the studies in social work education in terms of a particular model of professional socialisation that has been adopted and to suggest issues, including policy issues, which arise from this approach and which appear relevant to any form of contemporary inquiry into social work. It should be made clear that the model that has been used is not the only theoretical approach that is available and that other models would highlight different features of the process under review and suggest different issues for inquiry and discussion. Here there is a brief summary of the foregoing discussion in the book in terms of the model, and finally a discussion of certain specific issues arising from this.

The model (Bucher and Stelling, 1977)* distinguished

* R. Bucher and J. Stelling, 'Becoming Professional'. This book is the culmination of a long period of research on

between two levels: first, the structure of the socialising
programme (including the segmental affiliation of teachers,
the selection and assessment process) which set the scene
for the socialisation process; and, second, the situations
and experiences in which students and their teachers were
involved during training. The latter included students'
experiences of role playing and choice and use of role
models, and the stages of development which were experienced during training. The relationship between these two
levels involves the interplay between structural and situational variables in the sense that the former set the scene
for the situations in which socialisation takes place and
help determine the outcomes of socialisation.

It is clear that the segmental affiliations of social work
teachers have become more complex in recent years and that
the dominance of the therapeutic segment has been challenged by segments of a reformist or radical kind. While
these divisions are not clear cut, it is clear that there is
considerable disagreement and conflict over the nature of
social work education, not least a conflict between 'administrative' and 'academic' definitions (CCETSW, 1979).
This will have implications for the related processes of
selection and assessment, as well as for syllabus.
Generally, students will be faced with a more complex and
conflictful situation than in the past, including a tension
between differing definitions of client needs and therefore of
the nature of the skills and knowledge required. This conflict is shown particularly in the assessment process, in
which it has been argued that there is a reluctance to set
firm and realistic standards for students at the completion
of their course. This reflects the difficulties of defining
in any precise way the skills and knowledge relevant in
social work, as well as the difficult relationship between
fieldwork agencies and the social work courses. The
selection process has also been characterised by a conflict
between bureaucratic and professional norms.

Students' accounts of these experiences of social work
training, as well as the experience of conducting research
in this area, suggests that practice considerations are a

professional socialisation, and subsumes a number of previous publications, one of the most important of which is
R. Bucher (1965), The Psychiatric Residency and Professional Socialisation, 'Journal of Health and Human Behaviour', 6, 4.

dominant concern of both teachers and students and that
there is an early exposure to the realities of practice in
social work agencies. Practical training makes up at least
half of the total time spent by the student in his course.
This is reinforced by the adoption by a number of students
of fieldwork teacher models (or models which represent
practice) on which to fashion their own performances. One
effect of the dominance of practice is partially to insulate
the student from the college setting and to make the existence and effectiveness of student peer groups more difficult. Another effect that has been suggested is that the
close contact with practice and the nature of agency supervision is such as to 'neutralise' the issues in which the
students are involved in their practice, and to reduce the
critical nature of the student's reaction to his course of
training and to his growing identity as a professional social
worker (Pearson, 1973; Piven and Cloward, 1976).

Thus the progress of the student through the course is not
uneventful. Although for some the course may seem to have
little personal or even occupational significance, for others
there is a growing realisation that they are confronted with
a recognisable professional culture, embodied mainly in the
figures of college and fieldwork teachers, that eventually
must be adapted to or 'settled for' in some form. Such
adaptations can encompass a wide range of responses,
including 'rejections' and 'fronting' as well as the internalisation of professional norms, and this account has laid
stress on the student as an active agent in the socialisation
process. A feature of this process is the receipt by the
student of cues as to the success of his performance in
academic and fieldwork contexts both from teachers and other
other figures but also as 'self-generated' cues. Research
in other training programmes suggests that a feature of this
situation is the 'discounting' of many cues from others and
an early reliance on self-generated cues, and that the professional identity of the student may in some cases be formed
at rather an early stage in training. Thus the 'self-direct-
ing' student will pose important dilemmas for the profession
and its attempt to exercise control over its members, not
least because of the potentially insulating effect of reliance
on a professional self which has been generated in this way.
Occupational practices which are organised on rather individualistic principles (such as some 'front line' social work
organisations) can also sustain such an identity (Freidson,
1977).

The importance of the pioneering work of Bucher and
Stelling, apart from detailing the mechanism by which
socialisation actually occurs, lies in outlining the likely
effects of professional segments on training. One element
which is under-developed in this model is the process by
which such segments are produced and the nature of the
wider structural constraints that have generated the segments. There is probably less recognition than there
could be of the extent to which professional communities
have been penetrated by political and ideological controversies in the world outside the profession. It is also
necessary to add to the model a greater recognition
of the intervention of the state into most professional processes, including that of professional education.

(2) ISSUES IN SOCIAL WORK EDUCATION

The dominant position of social work teachers in the formation and interpretation of the teaching, selection and assessment programmes means that the nature of the recruitment to
this professional elite is of the greatest importance. The
'elevation' of college teachers to academic positions has
also given rise to problems for some students in their search
for models on which to base their own conception of professional practice. This has meant a leaning among students
towards fieldwork teachers and agencies as a primary
source of skills and knowledge, and a concern has arisen
that academic elements of courses are becoming less focused
in this latter direction and more concerned with general
education, particularly of a sociological kind (CCETSW,
1977). One response to this problem has been an attempt
to achieve a closer relationship between academic teachers
and practice, and part-time appointments for teachers in
social work agencies. For various reasons, particularly
the bureaucratic scheduling of organisations such as institutions of higher education and social work agencies, this
has been difficult to achieve and it is also argued that social
work teachers should define their interests outside teaching
as something other than a concern for practice, particularly
in the development of research (Cheetham, 1967). But
another alternative is the transformation of existing sociological teaching, which is often seen as irrelevant to practice as such, into a form of practice knowledge, where, for
example, the aim is to develop non-pathological accounts of

clients' 'problems' or 'situations' to set alongside other
accounts which may be invoked in practice (Evans and Webb,
1977). This also implies the breakdown of the distinction
between social work teachers (and other so called 'clinical'
teachers) and 'non-clinical teachers' (mainly social scientists) and the direct involvement of the latter in the teaching
of social work methods, as well as human growth and
development courses.

This also implies that departments of social work training, like American schools of social work, should support
the recruitment of specialist staff other than social workers
at all levels in the academic hierarchy, including the most
senior. Against this, it is argued that those without qualifications in social work should not hold such positions
because it undermines professionalism in the sense that such
persons are not able to provide appropriate leadership in
departments given over to the education of practitioners.
But it can also be held that such disadvantages are out-
weighed by the additional skills brought to the departments
by such appointments, particularly in research and in its
contribution to the development of social work knowledge,
and by the opportunity to provide students with a wider
range of role models than is otherwise the case. For a
number of reasons, including the burden of administrative
work, social work teachers have not until recently been
able to involve themselves in research activities to any
significant extent. As an editorial ('Times Higher
Educational Supplement', 30 June 1978) has suggested

> Social work is a highly individual occupation involving
> complicated personal and political judgements. Its prac-
> titioners must draw on a variety of experience and disci-
> pline to inform their actions. This is the richness of
> social work: it ought not to be eroded by too militant a
> campaign for the stamp of professionalism.

Another issue is the relationship between social work
education and the educational institutions in which this is
carried on. In chapter 3 the history of the difficult relationship between social work and the universities was outlined. The culture of social work education is somewhat
different from that of the universities, and particularly their
tradition of independence from external control, for example
in such matters as assessment and the routine intervention
of external training councils. For this reason it has been
argued that the universities are less appropriate places for
this form of education than colleges (such as polytechnics)

which are more accustomed to such intervention and where
there is a greater tradition of occupational education and
training.

Another argument stresses that existing educational
institutions (whether universities or polytechnics), which
have a virtual monopoly of this field, are alike in producing
graduates who have an education which has emphasised
general, social science type learning at the expense of
specific skills and knowledge, and that social work students
would receive a more relevant education if they emerged
from specialist colleges like those used for training police
inspectors or assistant governors in the prison service and
(in the past) for training teachers (Davies, 1979b). Not only
would such colleges be able to offer a range of specialisms
beyond the resources of most CQSW courses, but 'they
would operate more or less firmly under the control of the
profession and its agencies' (ibid.).

A further argument in favour of such a scheme is that of
the relation between the segmental organisation of social
work teachers, the small-scale nature of many courses and
the implications this has for the socialisation of the students.
If courses are small and the number of teachers therefore
limited, the opportunities clearly exist for a particular segment to colonise and even capture a particular course.
Only the most well-informed student will be aware of the
segmental affiliations of teachers on particular courses,
and thus students in general cannot know what they are about
to receive when they enter courses (ibid.).

This situation is for some contemporary critics of social
work education an illustration of the illegitimate merging of
the 'personal' and the 'political' elements in training
(Halmos, 1978). The balance between these dual elements
is threatened by the capture of particular courses by those
with specific segmental affiliations. The 'personalist'
approach, in which there is a primary concern and care for
the individual, is threatened by the 'political' redefinition of
this relationship and the context in which it goes on. This
is particularly the case in areas such as community work,
in which there is less of an established body of knowledge
than in other areas of social work. Departments of social
work training have in particular been faced with the dilemma
of those who deny the personal/political distinction, and the
consequent affect this might have on the training programme
(ibid.):

who shall define the values of these programmes and what

opportunities for dissent will be afforded to students? In the curricula of community work training, will students receive a variety of ideological orientations from a variety of teachers, or will the department or the school determine what political procedures tactics and ideological precepts shall be the substance and framework of the course.

Clearly one possible solution to this problem would be the establishment of larger courses in specialist training institutions where there is more likelihood of a variety of segmental and ideological affiliations together with a greater measure of professional control.

But the arguments against such a basic change in the organisation of social work education are probably convincing (Davies, 1979b). It is clear that the professions have benefited from the relationship with prestigious educational institutions and the variety of opportunities that are available, for example the emphasis on research and the development of knowledge as well as the passing on of knowledge.   The isolated circumstances of specialist institutions make it less likely that such opportunities are available, or that a solution to the domination of training programmes by particular segments will necessarily follow.   But this puts greater pressure on the established institutions to seek solutions to the problems of segmental affiliations and domination by re-emphasising the ideal of critical scrutiny of any claim to such dominance.

One problem that persists in the case of social work is that the differences in the prestige of educational institutions will serve to locate and give status to students who are successful in terms of qualifications and future careers, even where basic training has been largely standardised (Larson, 1977).   Crucial variations in the status and prestige attached to different forms of training will clearly weaken claims to professional status.   The distinctions between the status attached to social work training in universities, polytechnics and other colleges have often been glossed over by assertions of equality (Younghusband, 1978). It is also the case that the university and technical college students in my own original research exhibited greater similarities than differences when some of the outcomes of training were considered.

But the qualifications received by graduate and non-graduate students are probably not always awarded the same status by employers, while the non-graduate qualification

has no occupational currency outside the social work field
and therefore has a 'trapping' effect for its holders.

Selection and assessment can be seen within the same
context and the questions surrounding them relate to some
of the most basic issues concerning professionalism, notably
the 'inherent' conflict between bureaucratic and professional control.   But the relationship between bureaucracy
and the professions is not, as is frequently depicted, in all
cases one of conflict, and in social work in particular there
is considerable congruence between bureaucratic and professional criteria;   concepts such as organisational professionalism (Larson, 1977) or bureau-professionalism (Parry
and Parry, 1979) have been developed to express this relationship.   Bureaucracy and professionalism have, for
example, both been seen as sub-types of a wider category,
that of 'rational administration' (Stinchcombe, 1959).   In
social work the 'unity of school and field' is a generalisation
that is widely held, and is based upon the fact that social
work courses are reliant on social work agencies for the
practical training of students.   But the social work agency
may be part of a wider administrative structure (the local
authority) which not only employs social workers but sup-
ports and funds some of the institutions in which they are
trained.   It is hardly surprising that a conflict between
bureaucratic and professional norms should have arisen in
the form of what has become known as the Vyas case, which
was discussed more fully in chapter 6 on the selection of
students.   Here, while the bureaucratic/professional conflict was clearly revealed, it is arguable that the solution
adopted and the principles inherent in such a solution owed
much to the idea of 'administrative rationality' inherent in
both bureaucratic and professional values (Parsloe, 1979).

Like other professions, social work attempts to assess
not only academic knowledge but the application of this knowledge in practice situations.   In this sense, assessment of
knowledge is part of the more general conception and social
organisation of knowledge represented by the courses, and
assessment is the only feature of social work knowledge
that has been directly discussed in this book.

The discussion of assessment so far suggests that, as in
the case of selection, social work teachers attempt to
balance a concern for the applicant/student, expressed as
an attempt to treat students as individuals who are at different points in their development and who should be encouraged
to participate in their own education and evaluation, with a

concern to maintain professional standards of service
offered to the client.   One study has stressed the attention
given to the assessment 'process' and the concern with the
development of the student compared to the assessment
'event', implying the possibility of student failure to achieve
a final professional award (Brandon and Davies, 1979).
But it has also been shown that social work tutors, unlike
other groups who are involved, do in fact put the maintenance of professional standards first in assessing students
(Morrell, 1979b).   Apart from the difficulty of defining the
social work task, and therefore the exact nature of 'professional standards', it has been suggested that there is a conflict between the principles of student involvement and of
professional accountability that are being pursued by
teachers, and that this is inherent in the structure and
culture of socialising programmes.   If the student is
encouraged to be an active agent in his own socialisation
and evaluation, and this is combined with formal assessment
without the former being seen within the context of the
latter, the danger of the assessment process taking prece-
dence over the assessment event is very real.   If this
occurs, the renewal of the contract between the profession
and society which professional training represents is
threatened.

While there has been a general shift in higher education
towards a more critical and student centred approach
which is unlikely to be reversed, in social work it seems
likely that in future the demands of professionalism, particularly as represented by practice agencies, will be for a
more realistic balance between the needs of students and
the requirements of practice as well as between academic
and practical work (see the responses of the practice agencies to the CCETSW document, 1977; CCETSW, 1979).
The recent proposed changes in assessment requirements
on the part of CCETSW are a clear indication of this trend
(CCETSW, 1980b).   But it is also interesting to note that
the issue of the professional compared to the personal
development of the student is still a very important one,
and there remains a strong feeling on the part of some
teachers that the latter is a necessary and important feature
of professional identity and education (CCETSW, 1979).

Another important feature of the assessment system,
which merits further research attention, is that of 'discounting'.   Although demonstrated in the context of other forms
of professional training, it is also something that appears to

be implicit in the Brandon and Davies (1979) study of social
work assessment, in which it was clear that some assessment schemes allowed students to neutralise and even avoid
the consequence of assessment initiatives.

The discounting process suggests that professional
socialisation can fall rather short of its aim of making
students, and future practitioners, sensitive to the monitor-
ing and control functions of their own professional
colleagues and underlines a critique of the professions
previously expressed by Freidson (1970) that professionals
cannot in all circumstances be held accountable to their own
colleagues of the needs of the wider society. Here the
importance of a generally critical educational environment
is underlined; as Freidson (1977) puts it, educational programmes should

> make constructive criticisms and responsiveness to criti-
> cisms a ubiquitous part of the instructional process ...
> for the faculty as well as for students. Unless they
> /students/ are able to observe their instructors in situa-
> tions in which they receive criticism and respond to it
> productively, how can they be expected to adopt that mode
> of response themselves?

Studies within a variety of socialising programmes suggest that the experiences of students can be seen in terms of
a number of stages of development in which problems previously largely unknown to the student are encountered and
which are a function of the socialising programme and its
agents. This represents one of the most important features
of the climate of uncertainty with which the student has to
deal. At the same time, the attempts to apprehend and
overcome such problems are related to changes in the perception by students both of their courses and of themselves.
The importance of this process has sometimes received less
recognition than was its due, both by sociologists research-
ing in this field (this is accepted, for example, by Bucher
and Stelling (1977) in respect of their earlier work) and by
professional educators themselves. For example, if training programmes have, as seems likely, certain specified
effects, then it would seem reasonable for students to be
made aware that they are likely to experience such effects
and that training is likely to proceed in terms of the experience and resolution of such problems. It also seems possible
that students are reluctant to accept that they might change
in ways neither desired nor anticipated and they may consequently reject this kind of information even if it is offered to
them (ibid.).

Uncertainties are inevitable in professional training and learning to respond to uncertainty is an important part of such training. But if such training is to be based on more rational criteria, particularly if students are to retain some control over their own progress and to maintain support for their own position at times of 'crisis' in personal and professional development, the provision of this kind of information might well be considered an important part of the educational programme. One danger here is that the unexpected effects of professional training may be seen as a negative reference point against which both the training experience and future professional development may be viewed.

One response to the difficulties and problems experienced by students has been the setting up of 'contracts' between teacher and student. This has developed partly as a means of individualising the course for students, including both academic and fieldwork; in both cases this implies an agreement on the amount and type of work a student will undertake, and has evolved partly from the idea of short-term contracts between social workers and their clients. A feature of this process is that educational expectations can be set out for both teacher and student, and that students should take responsibility for their own learning and development. This can form a complement to continuous and other forms of assessment, and provide a more manageable and defined context in which assessment can take place (Parsloe, 1978; Robinson, 1978). Such contracts also illustrate the way in which certain principles utilised in relation to clients are incorporated (often without sufficient appreciation of the difficulties involved) into the teaching and learning process (Righton, 1979).

The process of socialisation and the variety of outcomes for the individual student throws further light upon the conflict between professional and bureaucratic modes of organisation. The issue is usually expressed as one of conflict between those individuals who have been exposed to the cognitive knowledge basis of a profession and are employed in organisations where such knowledge, and the autonomy which stems from it, are not accorded such recognition or importance. Professional employees are therefore potentially in a situation of considerable strain and conflict.

But the facts of professional socialisation challenge this picture, and social work seems a particularly good example of this; the variety of available pathways through the socialising programme and the variety of responses and

outcomes relating to that system means that professional
socialisation is far from a unitary process. Larson (1977)
has commented on the demystifying effects of empirical
studies on the accepted connotations of professionalism,
stressing 'the variety of motives that guide choice of professional career ... the diverse personalities that emerge
from professional training and the processes of educational
stratification and self selection.' It should also not be
forgotten that professional socialisation goes on in bureau-
cratised educational institutions, and therefore the budding
professional is exposed to the tactics and ideology of other
professionals in their attempts to perpetuate professionalism.

(3) CONCLUSION

To enter the field of social work education is to cross a
minefield of conjecture, refutation, claims and counter
claims. But the considerable tradition of research in the
sociology and social psychology of the occupations and professions can provide at least a starting-point for a more
rational appraisal of the issues involved. Here a particular model of professional socialisation has been used in an
attempt to put in perspective a number of small-scale
research projects. Such projects, by themselves, represent little more than small slices of experience seen through
the eyes of particular observers and productive mainly of
further issues and questions for research. The difficulties
of research in the area of professional socialisation are
considerable, and reflect both the jealously guarded inner
sanctum of a profession and the reluctance of students to
participate in an atmosphere of uncertainty and challenge to
themselves (see Michael, 1976, for an interesting account of
the rewards and difficulties of this kind of research in one
social work course).
    In the early part of this century Abraham Flexner toured
American medical schools and as a result publicised the
numerous departures from accepted standards of medical
education that he found (Flexner, 1910). If a modern Flexner were to make a similar tour of British schools and
departments of social work training today, a heroic project
in itself, it is interesting to speculate on the conclusions to
which he would come at a time of stress and change. Certainly the kinds of conditions that gave weight to Flexner's
original revelations (private knowledge made public), is not

relevant to social work today for both professional and now
public attention is increasingly focused on issues of skills,
competence and training.   There is little evidence of a
closing of professional ranks to avoid such discussion, as
suggested by Brewer and Lait (1980).   Yet if real changes
are to come about in professional practice and pressures for
this to be expressed in policy terms, they must surely have
their source in the educational processes by which professionals are produced.   While introspection is painful for
any profession, and not a notable accompaniment to most
professional activity, the current exchange of views,
opinions and attitudes in social work education among training administrators, teachers in academic and fieldwork
positions and students, is surely an indication of social
health rather than pathology.   Changes will occur in the
nature of social work education and this process can be
assisted by a responsible, critical sociology.   It is with
this end in view that this book has been conceived and on
which its usefulness may be judged.

Bibliography

AJS   'American Journal of Sociology'
App. Soc. Studs 'Applied Social Studies'
ASR   'American Sociological Review'
BJPSW   'British Journal of Psychiatric Social
              Work'
BJS   'British Journal of Sociology'
BJSW   'British Journal of Social Work'
CSWE   'Contemporary Social Work Education'
JESW   'Journal of Education for Social Work'
JHHB   'Journal of Health and Human Behaviour'
JHSB   'Journal of Health and Social Behaviour'
SWT   'Social Work Today'

ANON. (1968), Sociology and Social Work; a Student's
Dilemma, 'Child Care News', November.
BAILEY, R. and BRAKE, M. (eds) (1975), 'Radical Social
Work', London, Edward Arnold.
BASW (1977), 'The Social Work Task'.
BECKER, H. (1971), 'Sociological Work', London, Allen
Lane.
BECKER, H. and CARPER, J. (1956), Elements of Identi-
fication with an Occupation, ASR, 23, 1.
BECKER, H. and GEER, B. (1958), The Fate of Idealism
in the Medical School, ASR, 23, 1.
BECKER, H. et al. (1961), 'Boys in White', University of
Chicago Press.
BECKER, H. (ed.) (1966), 'Institutions and the Person',
University of Chicago Press.
BLAU, P. and SCOTT, W. (1962), 'Formal Organisations',
San Francisco, Chandler.
BOEHM, W. (1976), Social Work Education; Issues and

Problems in the Light of Recent Developments, JESW, Winter.

BOX, S. and FORD, J. (1967), Commitment to Science; a Solution to Student Marginality, 'Sociology', 1, 3.

BRANDON, J. and DAVIES, M. (1979), The Limits of Competence in Social Work, BJSW, 9, 3.

BREWER, C. and LAIT, J. (1980), 'Can Social Work Survive?', London, Temple Smith.

BRIM, O. (1968), Adult Socialisation, in J. Clausen (ed.), 'Socialisation and Society', Boston, Little Brown.

BROOM, L. and SMITH, J. (1967), Bridging Occupations, BJS, 14, 4.

BROWN, A. and WEBB, C. (1973), Social Work Teachers and Social Work Practice, BJSW, 3, 1.

BUCHER, R. (1965), The Psychiatric Residency and Professional Socialization, JHHB, 6, Winter.

BUCHER, R. and STELLING, J. (1977), 'Becoming Professional', London, Sage Publications.

BUCHER, R. and STRAUSS, A. (1961), Professions in Process, AJS, 66, 4.

BUTLER, B. (1968), Social Values and Social Work in the U.K., International Conference on Social Welfare.

CCETSW (1975), Education and Training for Social Work, discussion paper no. 10.

CCETSW (1977), Expectations of the Teaching of Social Work in Courses Leading to CQSW, consultative document 3.

CCETSW (1979), Expectations of the Teaching of Social Work in Courses Leading to CQSW; Analysis of Responses and Some Policy Issues Arising from the Consultation.

CCETSW (1980a), On Training for the Social Services.

CCETSW (1980b), The Assessment of Students for the Award of CQSW and the Nature and Length of Assessable Practice Placements.

CHEETHAM, J. (1967), From Social Work to Teaching; the First Year, 'Case Conference', 14, 8.

COLLISON, P. and KENNEDY, J. (1977), Graduate Recruits to Social Work, 'Social and Economic Administration', 11, 2.

COMMITTEE ON LOCAL AUTHORITY AND ALLIED PERSONAL SOCIAL SERVICES (Seebohm Committee) (1968), HMSO, CMND 3703, London.

CORRIGAN, P. and LEONARD, P. (1978), 'Social Work Practice Under Capitalism; a Marxist Approach', London, Macmillan.

COTGROVE, S. and BOX, S. (1970), 'Science, Industry and Society', London, Allen & Unwin.

COWLEY, J. et al. (eds) (1977), 'Community or Class
Struggle', London, Stage One Press.
COXON, A. (1965), A Sociological Study of the Social
Recruitment, Selection and Professional Socialization of
Anglican Ordinals, University of Leeds, PhD, unpublished.
CURNOCK, K. (1975), Student Units in Social Work Educa-
tion, CCETSW, paper 11.
CYPHER, J. (1975), Social Reform and the Social Work
Profession. What Hope for Rapprochement?, in H. Jones
(ed.), 'Towards a New Social Work', London, Routledge &
Kegan Paul.
DAVIES, E. (1973), The Use of T Groups in Training
Social Workers, BJSW, 3, 1.
DAVIES, M. (1979a), Improving the Quality of Assessment,
'Community Care', 27 September.
DAVIES, M. (1979b), The Shape of Things to Come, 'Com-
munity Care', 4 October.
DAVIS, F. (1968), Professional Socialisation as Subjec-
tive Experience, in Becker, H. (ed.) (1966).
DINGWALL, R. (1977), 'The Social Organisation of Health
Visitor Training', London, Croom Helm.
DONNISON, D. (1975), 'Social Policy and Administration
Revisited', London, Allen & Unwin.
DONNISON, D. (1979), Training for Social Work, SWT,
10, 4.
EDWARDS, M. (1971), Selection Interviews in Relation to
the Process of Reaching Admissions Decisions in School of
Social Work: Report of a Survey, App. Soc. Studs, 3.
EDWARDS, M. and FOSTER, G. (1980), The Interview in
Selection for Social Work Education, BJSW, 10, 3.
ELLIOTT, P. (1972), 'Sociology of the Professions',
London, Macmillan.
ELLIS, J. (1975), Selecting Students for Social Work
Training, BJSW, 5, 2.
EPSTEIN, I. (1970), Professionalization, Professionalism
and Social Worker Radicalism, JHSB, 11, 1.
EVANS, R. and WEBB, D. (1977), Sociology and Social
Work Practice; Explanation, or Method?, CSWE, 1, 2.
FLEXNER, A. (1910), Medical Education in the U.S. and
Canada; a Report to the Carnegie Foundation, New York.
FOX, R. (1957), Training for Uncertainty, in Merton, R.
et al. (1957)
FREIDSON, E. (1970), 'Profession of Medicine', New
York, Dodd Mead.
FREIDSON, E. (1973), Professionalization and the Organ-

ization of Middle Class Labour in Post Industrial Society, in Halmos (1973).

FREIDSON, E. (1977), Preface to Bucher and Stelling (1977).

GIBSON, R. (1978), From Whom do Teachers Learn the Role of Teachers?; the Reference Groups of Student Teachers, 'Research Intelligence', 3, 2.

GLASNER, P. (1977), 'Sociology of Secularization; Critique of a Concept', London, Routledge & Kegan Paul.

GOFFMAN, E. (1961), 'Asylums', Harmondsworth, Penguin.

GOODE, W. (1957), Community Within a Community; the Professions, ASR, 22.

HAMILTON, G. (1954), Self Awareness in Professional Education, 'Social Casework', 35.

HALMOS, P. (1978), 'The Personal and the Political', London, Hutchinson.

HALMOS, P. (ed.) (1973), 'Professionalization and Social Change', Keele University, Sociological Review Monograph no. 20.

HALSEY, A. (ed.) (1976), 'Traditions of Social Policy', Oxford, Blackwell.

HARRIS, J. (1977), 'William Beveridge; a Biography', Oxford, Clarendon Press.

HAYES, D. and VARLEY, B. (1965), Impact of Social Work Education on Students' Values, 'Social Work' (US), 27, 2.

HAYWARD, C. (1979), 'A Fair Assessment', CCETSW study no. 2.

HERAUD, B. (1970), 'Sociology and Social Work: Perspectives and Problems', Oxford, Pergamon.

HERAUD, B. (1972), Professionalization in Social Work; A Comparative Study of the Professional Socialization of Social Work Students in a University and Technical College Course, University of London, PhD, unpublished.

HERAUD, B. (1973), Professionalism, Radicalism and Social Change, in Halmos, P. (ed.) (1973).

HOLLOWAY, S. (1964), Medical Education in England, 1830-1858; a Sociological Analysis, 'History', vol. 49.

HUGHES, E. (1958), 'Men and Their Work', Chicago, Free Press.

JACKSON, J. (ed.) (1970), 'Professions and Professionalization', London, Cambridge University Press.

JACKSON, B. and MARSDEN, D. (1962), 'Education and the Working Class', London, Routledge & Kegan Paul.

JAMOUS, H. and PELOILLE, B. (1970), Professions or Self Perpetuating Systems: Changes in the French Hospital System, in Jackson, J. (1970).

JANOVITZ, M. (1960), 'The Professional Soldier',
Chicago, Free Press.
JEFFERYS, M. (1965), 'An Anatomy of Social Welfare
Services', London, Joseph.
JOHNSON, T. (1976), People and Work; Work and Power,
Open University Course DE. 351, Unit 16.
JOHNSON, T. (1977), The Professions in the Class Struc-
ture, in Scase, R. (1977).
JONES, H. (ed.) (1975), 'Towards a New Social Work',
London, Routledge & Kegan Paul.
JONES, K. (1964), The Teaching of Social Studies in
British Universities, 'Occasional Papers in Social Admin-
istration', no. 12, Codicote Press.
JONES, N. (1970), Selection of Students for Social Work
Training, 'Social Work' (UK), 27, 3.
KEOGH, P. (1968), Reflections on a Two Year Child Care
Course, 'Child Care News', no. 80.
KUMAR, K. (1978), 'Prophecy and Progress', Harmonds-
worth, Penguin.
LACEY, C. (1977), 'The Socialization of Teachers',
London, Methuen.
LANDSBERG, G. (1967), The Graduate School of Social
Work as a Socialising Institution, MSW thesis, New York
University, School of Social Work, unpublished.
LARSON, M. (1977), 'The Rise of Professionalism, a
Sociological Analysis', University of California Press.
LAYCOCK, A. (1968), Attitude Change in Adult Students
During Social Work Training, 'Social Work' (UK), 25, 3.
LEES, R. (1971), Social Action, 'New Society', 18, 474.
MCDOUGALL, K. (1962), Thinking Aloud About Social Work
Training, 'Case Conference', 8, 10.
MCGUIRE, J. (1966), The Development of Identification
with the Role of Nurse, 'International Journal of Nursing
Studies', 3.
MATHEWS, M. (1978), 'The Social Work Mystique: Towards
a Sociology of Social Work', Berkeley, Banner Books.
MARSLAND, D. (1969), An Exploration of Professional
Socialisation; The College of Education and the School
Teachers Role, Society for Research into Higher Educa-
tion, 5th Annual Conference.
MAYER, J. and ROSENBLATT, A. (1974), Sources of
Stress Among Student Practitioners in Social Work; a
Sociological View, JESW, 10, 3.
MAYER, J. and ROSENBLATT, A. (1975a), Objectionable
Supervisory Styles; the Student's Point of View, 'Social
Work' (US), 20, 2.

MAYER, J. and ROSENBLATT, A. (1975b), Encounters
With Danger; Social Workers in the Ghetto, 'Sociology of
Work and Occupations', 2, 3.
MAYFIELD, E. (1964), The Selection Interview – a Re-evalua-
tion of Published Research, 'Personnel Psychology', vol. 17.
MERTON, R.K. et al. (ed.) (1957), 'The Student Physician',
Harvard University Press.
MEYER, H. (1967), Professionalization in Social Work
Today, in Thomas, E. (ed.) (1967).
MICHAEL, G. (1976), Content and Method in Fieldwork
Teaching, University of Edinburgh, PhD thesis, unpub-
lished.
MILLERSON, G. (1964), 'The Qualifying Associations',
London, Routledge & Kegan Paul.
MORRELL, E. (1979a), The Assessment of Fieldwork Place-
ments, MPhil. thesis, University of Leicester, School of
Social Work, unpublished.
MORRELL, E. (1979b), A Lesson in Assessment, 'Community
Care', 1 November.
NYMAN, J. (1968), On Being a Social Work Student, 'Case
Conference', 14 November.
OLESON, V. and WHITTAKER, E. (1968), 'The Silent
Dialogue', San Francisco, Jossey Bass.
OPPENHEIMER, M. (1973), The Proletarianization of the
Professional, in Halmos (ed.) (1973).
PARRY, N. and J. (1973), Power, Class and Occupational
Strategy, BSA Conference, unpublished.
PARRY, N. et al. (eds) (1979), 'Social Work, Welfare and
the State', London, Edward Arnold.
PARRY, N. and J. (1979), Social Work, Professionalism
and the State, in Parry, N. et al. (eds) (1979).
PARSLOE, P. (1978), The Use of Contracts on a Social
Work Course, in Stevenson, O. (ed.) (1978).
PARSLOE, P. (1979), Selection for Professional Training;
the English and the American Experience, BJSW, 9, 3.
PARSLOE, P. and STEVENSON, O. (1979), Social Work
Training: The Struggle for Excellence, 'Community Care',
8 November.
PAYNE, M. and DAWSON, J. (1979), Student Participation
in a Social Work Course, SWT, 10, 24.
PARSONS, T. (1951), 'The Social System', London, Rout-
ledge & Kegan Paul.
PEARSON, G. (1973), Social Work as the Privatized Solu-
tion of Public Ills, BJSW, 3, 2.
PEARSON, G. (1975a), 'The Deviant Imagination', London,
Macmillan.

PEARSON, G. (1975b), The Politics of Uncertainty; a
Study in the Socialization of the Social Worker, in Jones,
H. (ed.) (1975).
PETTES, D. (1979), 'Staff and Student Supervision',
London, Allen & Unwin.
PINS, A. (1967), Who Chooses Social Work, When and Why?,
New York Council on Social Work Education.
PIVEN, F. and CLOWARD, R. (1976), Notes Towards a
Radical Social Work, in Bailey, R. and Brake, M. (eds)
(1975).
PRITCHARD, C. and TAYLOR, R. (1978), 'Social Work:
Reform or Revolution?', London, Routledge & Kegan Paul.
RICHARDS, M. and RIGHTON, P. (eds) (1979), 'Social
Work Education in Conflict', NISW paper 10.
RIGHTON, P. (1979), Knowledge About Teaching and Learn-
ing in Social Work Education, in Richards, M. and Righton,
P. (eds) (1979).
ROBINSON, M. (1978), Contract Making in Social Work
Practice, in Stevenson, O. (ed.) (1978).
ROSEN, A. (1970), Can Schools Survive the Current
Crisis?, 'Social Work Education Reporter', 18, 2.
ROTHBLATT, S. (1968), 'The Revolution Among the Dons,
Cambridge and Society in Victorian England', London,
Faber & Faber.
RUSTIN, M. (1971), Structural and Unconscious Implica-
tions of the Dyad and Triad, 'Sociological Review', 19.
SCASE, R. (ed.) (1977), 'Industrial Society: Class,
Cleavage and Control', London, Allen & Unwin.
SHEARER, A. (1979), An Analysis of the Role and Effec-
tiveness of CCETSW, SWT, 10, 24
SCHUTZ, A. (1964), 'Collected Papers', vol. 2, The
Hague, Nijhoff.
SCHUTZ, A. and LUCKMANN, T. (1974), 'The Structures
of the Life World', London, Heinemann.
SEED, P. (1973), 'The Expansion of Social Work in
Britain', London, Routledge & Kegan Paul.
SHEY, T. (1968), Professional Socialization in Social
Work, New School for Social Research, New York, PhD,
unpublished.
SHIPMAN, M. (1966), Personal and Social Influences in
the Work of a Teachers Training College, University of
London, PhD thesis, unpublished.
SIMPSON, I. (1967), Patterns of Socialization into Profes-
sion; the Case of Student Nurses, 'Social Inquiry', 37.
SPARROW, J. (1978), 'Diary of a Student Social Worker',
London, Routledge & Kegan Paul.

STEVENSON, O. (1976), The Development of Social Work
Education, in Halsey, A. (ed.) (1976).
STEVENSON, O. (ed.) (1978), 'Trends in Social Work
Education', Association of Teachers in Social Work, paper
11.
STEVENSON, O. and PARSLOE, P. (1978), Social Service
Teams: The Practitioners' View, DHSS.
STINCHCOMBE, A. (1959), Bureaucratic and Craft Admin-
istration of Production, 'Administrative Science Quarter-
ly', 4.
STORR, A. (1979) 'The Art of Psycho-therapy', London,
Secker & Warburg.
TAYLOR, W. (1969), 'Society and the Education of
Teachers', London, Faber & Faber.
THOMAS, E. (ed.) (1967), 'Behavioural Science for Social
Workers', New York, Free Press.
'TIMES HIGHER EDUCATIONAL SUPPLEMENT' (1978),
Editorial, 30 June.
'TIMES' (1978), Law Report, 4 May.
TIMMS, N. (1964), 'Psychiatric Social Work in Britain',
London, Routledge & Kegan Paul.
TIMMS, N. (1970), 'Social Work: an Outline for the Intend-
ing Student', London, Routledge & Kegan Paul.
TITMUS, R. (1950), 'Problems of Social Policy', London,
HMSO
TITMUS, R. (1968), 'Commitment to Welfare', London,
Allen & Unwin.
TOWLE, C. (1967), 'The Learner in Education for the Pro-
fessions', University of Chicago Press.
UNITED NATIONS (1958), 'Training for Social Work',
Third International Survey, New York.   Cited in
Matthews, M. (1978).
VARLEY, B. (1968), Social Work Values; Changes in
Value Commitment of Students from Admission to MSW
Graduation, JESW, Fall.
WALDRON, F. (1959), Challenge to Professional Social
Work, 'Social Work' (UK), 16, 3.
WALTON, R. (1975), 'Women in Social Work', London,
Routledge & Kegan Paul.
WILENSKY, H. and LEBEAUX, C. (1965), 'Industrial
Society and Social Welfare', New York, Free Press.
WILKINSON, P. (1971), 'Social Movements', London Pall
Mall Press.
WILLCOCKS, A. (1959), The Younghusband Report, 'Case
Conference', 6. 3.

WILSON, E. (1977), Radical Social Work: Myth or Reality, in Cowley, J. et al. (eds) (1977).

WOODCOCK, G. (1966), Tutor, Supervisor and Student: an Evaluation of Roles in Social Work Training, BJPSW, 8, 3.

WOOTTON, B. (1959), Daddy Knows Best, 'Twentieth Century', October.

WRIGHT, R. (1961), A Challenge to Social Work Education, 'Case Conference', vol. 8, no. 20.

YOUNGHUSBAND, E. (1947), 'The Employment and Training of Social Workers', Dunfermline, Carnegie United Kingdom Trust.

YOUNGHUSBAND, E. (1959), 'Report of the Working Party on Social Workers in the Local Authority Health and Welfare Services', London, HMSO.

YOUNGHUSBAND, E. (1978), 'Social Work in Britain, 1950-75', vol. 2, London, Allen & Unwin.

Index

Routledge Social Science Series

Routledge & Kegan Paul   London, Henley and Boston

39 Store Street,
London WC1E 7DD
Broadway House,
Newtown Road,
Henley-on-Thames,
Oxon RG9 1EN
9 Park Street,
Boston, Mass. 02108

Contents

*Authors wishing to submit manuscripts for any series
in this catalogue should send them to the Social Science Editor,
Routledge & Kegan Paul Ltd, 39 Store Street,
London WC1E 7DD.*
● *Books so marked are available in paperback.*
○ *Books so marked are available in paperback only.*
*All books are in metric Demy 8vo format (216 × 138mm approx.)
unless otherwise stated.*

International Library of Sociology
General Editor John Rex

GENERAL SOCIOLOGY

Barnsley, J. H. The Social Reality of Ethics. *464 pp.*
Brown, Robert. Explanation in Social Science. *208 pp.*
● Rules and Laws in Sociology. *192 pp.*
Bruford, W. H. Chekhov and His Russia. *A Sociological Study. 244 pp.*
Burton, F. and **Carlen, P.** Official Discourse. *On Discourse Analysis, Government Publications, Ideology. About 140 pp.*
Cain, Maureen E. Society and the Policeman's Role. *326 pp.*
● **Fletcher, Colin.** Beneath the Surface. *An Account of Three Styles of Sociological Research. 221 pp.*
Gibson, Quentin. The Logic of Social Enquiry. *240 pp.*
Glassner, B. Essential Interactionism. *208 pp.*
Glucksmann, M. Structuralist Analysis in Contemporary Social Thought. *212 pp.*
Gurvitch, Georges. Sociology of Law. *Foreword by Roscoe Pound. 264 pp.*
Hinkle, R. Founding Theory of American Sociology 1881–1913. *About 350 pp.*
Homans, George C. Sentiments and Activities. *336 pp.*
Johnson, Harry M. Sociology: *A Systematic Introduction. Foreword by Robert K. Merton. 710 pp.*
● **Keat, Russell** and **Urry, John.** Social Theory as Science. *278 pp.*
Mannheim, Karl. Essays on Sociology and Social Psychology. *Edited by Paul Keckskemeti. With Editorial Note by Adolph Lowe. 344 pp.*
Martindale, Don. The Nature and Types of Sociological Theory. *292 pp.*
● **Maus, Heinz.** A Short History of Sociology. *234 pp.*
Myrdal, Gunnar. Value in Social Theory: *A Collection of Essays on Methodology. Edited by Paul Streeten. 332 pp.*
Ogburn, William F. and **Nimkoff, Meyer F.** A Handbook of Sociology. *Preface by Karl Mannheim. 656 pp. 46 figures. 35 tables.*
Parsons, Talcott and **Smelser, Neil J.** Economy and Society: *A Study in the Integration of Economic and Social Theory. 362 pp.*
Payne, G., Dingwall, R., Payne, J. and **Carter, M.** Sociology and Social Research. *About 250 pp.*
Podgórecki, A. Practical Social Sciences. *About 200 pp.*
Podgórecki, A. and **Łos, M.** Multidimensional Sociology. *268 pp.*
Raffel, S. Matters of Fact. *A Sociological Inquiry. 152 pp.*
● **Rex, John.** Key Problems of Sociological Theory. *220 pp.*
Sociology and the Demystification of the Modern World. *282 pp.*
● **Rex, John.** (Ed.) Approaches to Sociology. *Contributions by Peter Abell, Frank Bechhofer, Basil Bernstein, Ronald Fletcher, David Frisby, Miriam Glucksmann, Peter Lassman, Herminio Martins, John Rex, Roland Robertson, John Westergaard and Jock Young. 302 pp.*
Rigby, A. Alternative Realities. *352 pp.*
Roche, M. Phenomenology, Language and the Social Sciences. *374 pp.*
Sahay, A. Sociological Analysis. *220 pp.*
Strasser, Hermann. The Normative Structure of Sociology. *Conservative and Emancipatory Themes in Social Thought. About 340 pp.*
Strong, P. Ceremonial Order of the Clinic. *267 pp.*
Urry, John. Reference Groups and the Theory of Revolution. *244 pp.*
Weinberg, E. Development of Sociology in the Soviet Union. *173 pp.*

FOREIGN CLASSICS OF SOCIOLOGY

● **Gerth, H. H.** and **Mills, C. Wright.** From Max Weber: *Essays in Sociology. 502 pp.*

● **Tönnies, Ferdinand.** Community and Association *(Gemeinschaft und Gesell-schaft).\Translated and Supplemented by Charles P. Loomis. Foreword by Pitirim A. Sorokin. 334 pp.*

SOCIAL STRUCTURE

Andreski, Stanislav. Military Organization and Society. *Foreword by Professor A. R. Radcliffe-Brown. 226 pp. 1 folder.*
Broom, L., Lancaster Jones, F., McDonnell, P. and **Williams, T.** The Inheritance of Inequality. *About 180 pp.*
Carlton, Eric. Ideology and Social Order. *Foreword by Professor Philip Abrahams. About 320 pp.*
Clegg, S. and **Dunkerley, D.** Organization, Class and Control. *614 pp.*
Coontz, Sydney H. Population Theories and the Economic Interpretation. *202 pp.*
Coser, Lewis. The Functions of Social Conflict. *204 pp.*
Crook, I. and **D.** The First Years of the Yangyi Commune. *304 pp., illustrated.*
Dickie-Clark, H. F. Marginal Situation: *A Sociological Study of a Coloured Group. 240 pp. 11 tables.*
Giner, S. and **Archer, M. S.** (Eds) Contemporary Europe: *Social Structures and Cultural Patterns, 336 pp.*
● **Glaser, Barney** and **Strauss, Anselm L.** Status Passage: *A Formal Theory. 212 pp.*
Glass, D. V. (Ed.) Social Mobility in Britain. *Contributions by J. Berent, T. Bottomore, R. C. Chambers, J. Floud, D. V. Glass, J. R. Hall, H. T. Himmelweit, R. K. Kelsall, F. M. Martin, C. A. Moser, R. Mukherjee and W. Ziegel. 420 pp.*
Kelsall, R. K. Higher Civil Servants in Britain: *From 1870 to the Present Day. 268 pp. 31 tables.*
● **Lawton, Denis.** Social Class, Language and Education. *192 pp.*
McLeish, John. The Theory of Social Change: *Four Views Considered. 128 pp.*
● **Marsh, David C.** The Changing Social Structure of England and Wales, 1871–1961. *Revised edition. 288 pp.*
Menzies, Ken. Talcott Parsons and the Social Image of Man. *About 208 pp.*
● **Mouzelis, Nicos.** Organization and Bureaucracy. *An Analysis of Modern Theories. 240 pp.*
● **Ossowski, Stanislaw.** Class Structure in the Social Consciousness. *210 pp.*
● **Podgórecki, Adam.** Law and Society. *302 pp.*
Renner, Karl. Institutions of Private Law and Their Social Functions. *Edited, with an Introduction and Notes, by O. Kahn-Freud. Translated by Agnes Schwarzschild. 316 pp.*
Rex, J. and **Tomlinson, S.** Colonial Immigrants in a British City. *A Class Analysis. 368 pp.*
Smooha, S. Israel: Pluralism and Conflict. *472 pp.*
Wesolowski, W. Class, Strata and Power. *Trans. and with Introduction by G. Kolankiewicz. 160 pp.*
Zureik, E. Palestinians in Israel. *A Study in Internal Colonialism. 264 pp.*

SOCIOLOGY AND POLITICS

Acton, T. A. Gypsy Politics and Social Change. *316 pp.*
Burton, F. Politics of Legitimacy. *Struggles in a Belfast Community. 250 pp.*
Crook, I. and **D.** Revolution in a Chinese Village. *Ten Mile Inn. 216 pp., illustrated.*
Etzioni-Halevy, E. Political Manipulation and Administrative Power. *A Comparative Study. About 200 pp.*
Fielding, N. The National Front. *About 250 pp.*
● **Hechter, Michael.** Internal Colonialism. *The Celtic Fringe in British National Development, 1536–1966. 380 pp.*
Kornhauser, William. The Politics of Mass Society. *272 pp. 20 tables.*

Korpi, W. The Working Class in Welfare Capitalism. *Work, Unions and Politics in Sweden. 472 pp.*

Kroes, R. Soldiers and Students. *A Study of Right- and Left-wing Students. 174 pp.*

Martin, Roderick. Sociology of Power. *About 272 pp.*

Merquior, J. G. Rousseau and Weber. *A Study in the Theory of Legitimacy. About 288 pp.*

Myrdal, Gunnar. The Political Element in the Development of Economic Theory. *Translated from the German by Paul Streeten. 282 pp.*

Varma, B. N. The Sociology and Politics of Development. *A Theoretical Study. 236 pp.*

Wong, S.-L. Sociology and Socialism in Contemporary China. *160 pp.*

Wootton, Graham. Workers, Unions and the State. *188 pp.*

CRIMINOLOGY

Ancel, Marc. Social Defence: *A Modern Approach to Criminal Problems. Foreword by Leon Radzinowicz. 240 pp.*

Athens, L. Violent Criminal Acts and Actors. *104 pp.*

Cain, Maureen E. Society and the Policeman's Role. *326 pp.*

Cloward, Richard A. and **Ohlin, Lloyd E.** Delinquency and Opportunity: *A Theory of Delinquent Gangs. 248 pp.*

Downes, David M. The Delinquent Solution. *A Study in Subcultural Theory. 296 pp.*

Friedlander, Kate. The Psycho-Analytical Approach to Juvenile Delinquency: *Theory, Case Studies, Treatment. 320 pp.*

Gleuck, Sheldon and **Eleanor.** Family Environment and Delinquency. *With the statistical assistance of Rose W. Kneznek. 340 pp.*

Lopez-Rey, Manuel. Crime. *An Analytical Appraisal. 288 pp.*

Mannheim, Hermann. Comparative Criminology: *A Text Book. Two volumes. 442 pp. and 380 pp.*

Morris, Terence. The Criminal Area: *A Study in Social Ecology. Foreword by Hermann Mannheim. 232 pp. 25 tables. 4 maps.*

Rock, Paul. Making People Pay. *338 pp.*

● **Taylor, Ian, Walton, Paul** and **Young, Jock.** The New Criminology. *For a Social Theory of Deviance. 325 pp.*

● **Taylor, Ian, Walton, Paul** and **Young, Jock.** (Eds) Critical Criminology. *268 pp.*

SOCIAL PSYCHOLOGY

Bagley, Christopher. The Social Psychology of the Epileptic Child. *320 pp.*

Brittan, Arthur. Meanings and Situations. *224 pp.*

Carroll, J. Break-Out from the Crystal Palace. *200 pp.*

● **Fleming, C. M.** Adolescence: Its Social Psychology. *With an Introduction to recent findings from the fields of Anthropology, Physiology, Medicine, Psychometrics and Sociometry. 288 pp.*

● The Social Psychology of Education: *An Introduction and Guide to Its Study. 136 pp.*

Linton, Ralph. The Cultural Background of Personality. *132 pp.*

● **Mayo, Elton.** The Social Problems of an Industrial Civilization. *With an Appendix on the Political Problem. 180 pp.*

Ottaway, A. K. C. Learning Through Group Experience. *176 pp.*

Plummer, Ken. Sexual Stigma. *An Interactionist Account. 254 pp.*

● **Rose, Arnold M.** (Ed.) Human Behaviour and Social Processes: *an Interactionist Approach. Contributions by Arnold M. Rose, Ralph H. Turner, Anselm Strauss, Everett C. Hughes, E. Franklin Frazier, Howard S. Becker et al. 696 pp.*

Smelser, Neil J. Theory of Collective Behaviour. *448 pp.*

Stephenson, Geoffrey M. The Development of Conscience. *128 pp.*

Young, Kimball. Handbook of Social Psychology. *658 pp. 16 figures. 10 tables.*

SOCIOLOGY OF THE FAMILY

Bell, Colin R. Middle Class Families: *Social and Geographical Mobility. 224 pp.*
Burton, Lindy. Vulnerable Children. *272 pp.*
Gavron, Hannah. The Captive Wife: *Conflicts of Household Mothers. 190 pp.*
George, Victor and **Wilding, Paul.** Motherless Families. *248 pp.*
Klein, Josephine. Samples from English Cultures.
   1. Three Preliminary Studies and Aspects of Adult Life in England. *447 pp.*
   2. Child-Rearing Practices and Index. *247 pp.*
Klein, Viola. The Feminine Character. *History of an Ideology. 244 pp.*
McWhinnie, Alexina M. Adopted Children. *How They Grow Up. 304 pp.*
● **Morgan, D. H. J.** Social Theory and the Family. *About 320 pp.*
● **Myrdal, Alva** and **Klein, Viola.** Women's Two Roles: *Home and Work. 238 pp.*
   27 tables.
Parsons, Talcott and **Bales, Robert F.** Family: Socialization and Interaction Process.
   In collaboration with James Olds, Morris Zelditch and Philip E. Slater. 456 pp.
   50 figures and tables.

SOCIAL SERVICES

Bastide, Roger. The Sociology of Mental Disorder. *Translated from the French by*
   Jean McNeil. 260 pp.
Carlebach, Julius. Caring For Children in Trouble. *266 pp.*
George, Victor. Foster Care. *Theory and Practice. 234 pp.*
   Social Security: *Beveridge and After. 258 pp.*
George, V. and **Wilding, P.** Motherless Families. *248 pp.*
● **Goetschius, George W.** Working with Community Groups. *256 pp.*
Goetschius, George W. and **Tash, Joan.** Working with Unattached Youth. *416 pp.*
Heywood, Jean S. Children in Care. *The Development of the Service for the Deprived*
   Child. Third revised edition. 284 pp.
King, Roy D., Ranes, Norma V. and **Tizard, Jack.** Patterns of Residential Care.
   356 pp.
Leigh, John. Young People and Leisure. *256 pp.*
● **Mays, John.** (Ed.) Penelope Hall's Social Services of England and Wales.
   368 pp.
Morris, Mary. Voluntary Work and the Welfare State. *300 pp.*
Nokes, P. L. The Professional Task in Welfare Practice. *152 pp.*
Timms, Noel. Psychiatric Social Work in Great Britain (1939–1962). *280 pp.*
●   Social Casework: *Principles and Practice. 256 pp.*

SOCIOLOGY OF EDUCATION

Banks, Olive. Parity and Prestige in English Secondary Education: a Study in
   Educational Sociology. *272 pp.*
● **Blyth, W. A. L.** English Primary Education. *A Sociological Description.*
   2. Background. *168 pp.*
Collier, K. G. The Social Purposes of Education: *Personal and Social Values in*
   Education. 268 pp.
Evans, K. M. Sociometry and Education. *158 pp.*
● **Ford, Julienne.** Social Class and the Comprehensive School. *192 pp.*
Foster, P. J. Education and Social Change in Ghana. *336 pp. 3 maps.*
Fraser, W. R. Education and Society in Modern France. *150 pp.*
Grace, Gerald R. Role Conflict and the Teacher. *150 pp.*
Hans, Nicholas. New Trends in Education in the Eighteenth Century. *278 pp.*
   19 tables.
●   Comparative Education: *A Study of Educational Factors and Traditions. 360 pp.*
● **Hargreaves, David.** Interpersonal Relations and Education. *432 pp.*
●   Social Relations in a Secondary School. *240 pp.*
   School Organization and Pupil Involvement. *A Study of Secondary Schools.*

- **Mannheim, Karl** and **Stewart, W. A. C.** An Introduction to the Sociology of Education. *206 pp.*
- **Musgrove, F.** Youth and the Social Order. *176 pp.*
- **Ottaway, A. K. C.** Education and Society: An Introduction to the Sociology of Education. *With an Introduction by W. O. Lester Smith. 212 pp.*
  Peers, Robert. Adult Education: *A Comparative Study. Revised edition. 398 pp.*
  Stratta, Erica. The Education of Borstal Boys. *A Study of their Educational Experiences prior to, and during, Borstal Training. 256 pp.*
- **Taylor, P. H., Reid, W. A.** and **Holley, B. J.** The English Sixth Form. *A Case Study in Curriculum Research. 198 pp.*

SOCIOLOGY OF CULTURE

Eppel, E. M. and **M.** Adolescents and Morality: *A Study of some Moral Values and Dilemmas of Working Adolescents in the Context of a changing Climate of Opinion. Foreword by W. J. H. Sprott. 268 pp. 39 tables.*
- **Fromm, Erich.** The Fear of Freedom. *286 pp.*
- The Sane Society. *400 pp.*
  Johnson, L. The Cultural Critics. *From Matthew Arnold to Raymond Williams. 233 pp.*
  Mannheim, Karl. Essays on the Sociology of Culture. *Edited by Ernst Mannheim in co-operation with Paul Kecskemeti. Editorial Note by Adolph Lowe. 280 pp.*
  Merquior, J. G. The Veil and the Mask. *Essays on Culture and Ideology. Foreword by Ernest Gellner. 140 pp.*
  Zijderfeld, A. C. On Clichés. *The Supersedure of Meaning by Function in Modernity. 150 pp.*

SOCIOLOGY OF RELIGION

Argyle, Michael and **Beit-Hallahmi, Benjamin.** The Social Psychology of Religion. *256 pp.*
Glasner, Peter E. The Sociology of Secularisation. *A Critique of a Concept. 146 pp.*
Hall, J. R. The Ways Out. *Utopian Communal Groups in an Age of Babylon. 280 pp.*
Ranson, S., Hinings, B. and **Bryman, A.** Clergy, Ministers and Priests. *216 pp.*
Stark, Werner. The Sociology of Religion. *A Study of Christendom.*
  Volume II. *Sectarian Religion. 368 pp.*
  Volume III. *The Universal Church. 464 pp.*
  Volume IV. *Types of Religious Man. 352 pp.*
  Volume V. *Types of Religious Culture. 464 pp.*
Turner, B. S. Weber and Islam. *216 pp.*
Watt, W. Montgomery. Islam and the Integration of Society. *320 pp.*

SOCIOLOGY OF ART AND LITERATURE

Jarvie, Ian C. Towards a Sociology of the Cinema. *A Comparative Essay on the Structure and Functioning of a Major Entertainment Industry. 405 pp.*
Rust, Frances S. Dance in Society. *An Analysis of the Relationships between the Social Dance and Society in England from the Middle Ages to the Present Day. 256 pp. 8 pp. of plates.*
Schücking, L. L. The Sociology of Literary Taste. *112 pp.*
Wolff, Janet. Hermeneutic Philosophy and the Sociology of Art. *150 pp.*

SOCIOLOGY OF KNOWLEDGE

Diesing, P. Patterns of Discovery in the Social Sciences. *262 pp.*

● **Douglas, J. D.** (Ed.) Understanding Everyday Life. *370 pp.*
● **Hamilton, P.** Knowledge and Social Structure. *174 pp.*
  Jarvie, I. C. Concepts and Society. *232 pp.*
  Mannheim, Karl. Essays on the Sociology of Knowledge. *Edited by Paul Kecskemeti. Editorial Note by Adolph Lowe. 353 pp.*
  Remmling, Gunter W. The Sociology of Karl Mannheim. *With a Bibliographical Guide to the Sociology of Knowledge, Ideological Analysis, and Social Planning. 255 pp.*
  Remmling, Gunter W. (Ed.) Towards the Sociology of Knowledge. *Origin and Development of a Sociological Thought Style. 463 pp.*
  Scheler, M. Problems of a Sociology of Knowledge. *Trans. by M. S. Frings. Edited and with an Introduction by K. Stikkers. 232 pp.*

URBAN SOCIOLOGY

  Aldridge, M. The British New Towns. *A Programme Without a Policy. 232 pp.*
  Ashworth, William. The Genesis of Modern British Town Planning: *A Study in Economic and Social History of the Nineteenth and Twentieth Centuries. 288 pp.*
  Brittan, A. The Privatised World. *196 pp.*
  Cullingworth, J. B. Housing Needs and Planning Policy: *A Restatement of the Problems of Housing Need and 'Overspill' in England and Wales. 232 pp. 44 tables. 8 maps.*
  Dickinson, Robert E. City and Region: *A Geographical Interpretation. 608 pp. 125 figures.*
  The West European City: *A Geographical Interpretation. 600 pp. 129 maps. 29 plates.*
  Humphreys, Alexander J. New Dubliners: *Urbanization and the Irish Family. Foreword by George C. Homans. 304 pp.*
  Jackson, Brian. Working Class Community: *Some General Notions raised by a Series of Studies in Northern England. 192 pp.*
● **Mann, P. H.** An Approach to Urban Sociology. *240 pp.*
  Mellor, J. R. Urban Sociology In an Urbanized Society. *326 pp.*
  Morris, R. N. and **Mogey, J.** The Sociology of Housing. *Studies at Berinsfield. 232 pp 4 pp. plates.*
  Mullan, R. Stevenage Ltd. *About 250 pp.*
  Rex, J. and **Tomlinson, S.** Colonial Immigrants in a British City. *A Class Analysis. 368 pp.*
  Rosser, C. and **Harris, C.** The Family and Social Change. *A Study of Family and Kinship in a South Wales Town. 352 pp. 8 maps.*
● **Stacey, Margaret, Batsone, Eric, Bell, Colin** and **Thurcott, Anne.** Power, Persistence and Change. *A Second Study of Banbury. 196 pp.*

RURAL SOCIOLOGY

  Mayer, Adrian C. Peasants in the Pacific. *A Study of Fiji Indian Rural Society. 248 pp. 20 plates.*
  Williams, W. M. The Sociology of an English Village: *Gosforth. 272 pp. 12 figures. 13 tables.*

SOCIOLOGY OF INDUSTRY AND DISTRIBUTION

  Dunkerley, David. The Foreman. *Aspects of Task and Structure. 192 pp.*
  Eldridge, J. E. T. Industrial Disputes. *Essays in the Sociology of Industrial Relations. 288 pp.*
  Hollowell, Peter G. The Lorry Driver. *272 pp.*
● **Oxaal, I., Barnett, T.** and **Booth, D.** (Eds) Beyond the Sociology of Development.

8

Economy and Society in Latin America and Africa. 295 pp.

Smelser, Neil J. Social Change in the Industrial Revolution: *An Application of Theory to the Lancashire Cotton Industry, 1770–1840. 468 pp. 12 figures. 14 tables.*

Watson, T. J. The Personnel Managers. *A Study in the Sociology of Work and Employment, 262 pp.*

ANTHROPOLOGY

Brandel-Syrier, Mia. Reeftown Elite. *A Study of Social Mobility in a Modern African Community on the Reef. 376 pp.*

Dickie-Clark, H. F. The Marginal Situation. *A Sociological Study of a Coloured Group. 236 pp.*

Dube, S. C. Indian Village. *Foreword by Morris Edward Opler. 276 pp. 4 plates.*
India's Changing Villages: *Human Factors in Community Development. 260 pp. 8 plates. 1 map.*

Fei, H.-T. Peasant Life in China. *A Field Study of Country Life in the Yangtze Valley. With a foreword by Bronislaw Malinowski. 328 pp. 16 pp. plates.*

Firth, Raymond. Malay Fishermen. *Their Peasant Economy. 420 pp. 17 pp. plates.*

Gulliver, P. H. Social Control in an African Society: a Study of the Arusha, Agricultural Masai of Northern Tanganyika. *320 pp. 8 plates. 10 figures.*
Family Herds. *288 pp.*

Jarvie, Ian C. The Revolution in Anthropology. *268 pp.*

Little, Kenneth L. Mende of Sierra Leone. *308 pp. and folder.*
Negroes in Britain. *With a New Introduction and Contemporary Study by Leonard Bloom. 320 pp.*

Tambs-Lyche, H. London Patidars. *About 180 pp.*

Madan, G. R. Western Sociologists on Indian Society. *Marx, Spencer, Weber, Durkheim, Pareto. 384 pp.*

Mayer, A. C. Peasants in the Pacific. *A Study of Fiji Indian Rural Society. 248 pp.*

Meer, Fatima. Race and Suicide in South Africa. *325 pp.*

Smith, Raymond T. The Negro Family in British Guiana: *Family Structure and Social Status in the Villages. With a Foreword by Meyer Fortes. 314 pp. 8 plates. 1 figure. 4 maps.*

SOCIOLOGY AND PHILOSOPHY

Adriaansens, H. Talcott Parsons and the Conceptual Dilemma. *About 224 pp.*

Barnsley, John H. The Social Reality of Ethics. *A Comparative Analysis of Moral Codes. 448 pp.*

Diesing, Paul. Patterns of Discovery in the Social Sciences. *362 pp.*

● **Douglas, Jack D.** (Ed.) Understanding Everyday Life. *Toward the Reconstruction of Sociological Knowledge. Contributions by Alan F. Blum, Aaron W. Cicourel, Norman K. Denzin, Jack D. Douglas, John Heeren, Peter McHugh, Peter K. Manning, Melvin Power, Matthew Speier, Roy Turner, D. Lawrence Wieder, Thomas P. Wilson and Don H. Zimmerman. 370 pp.*

Gorman, Robert A. The Dual Vision. *Alfred Schutz and the Myth of Phenomenological Social Science. 240 pp.*

Jarvie, Ian C. Concepts and Society. *216 pp.*

Kilminster, R. Praxis and Method. *A Sociological Dialogue with Lukács, Gramsci and the Early Frankfurt School. 334 pp.*

● **Pelz, Werner.** The Scope of Understanding in Sociology. *Towards a More Radical Reorientation in the Social Humanistic Sciences. 283 pp.*

Roche, Maurice. Phenomenology, Language and the Social Sciences. *371 pp.*

Sahay, Arun. Sociological Analysis. *212 pp.*

● **Slater, P.** Origin and Significance of the Frankfurt School. *A Marxist Perspective. 185 pp.*

Spurling, L. Phenomenology and the Social World. *The Philosophy of Merleau-Ponty and its Relation to the Social Sciences. 222 pp.*

Wilson, H. T. The American Ideology. *Science, Technology and Organization as Modes of Rationality. 368 pp.*

International Library of Anthropology
General Editor Adam Kuper

● Ahmed, A. S. Millennium and Charisma Among Pathans. *A Critical Essay in Social Anthropology. 192 pp.*
Pukhtun Economy and Society. *Traditional Structure and Economic Development. About 360 pp.*

Barth, F. Selected Essays. *Volume I. About 250 pp.* Selected Essays. *Volume II. About 250 pp.*

Brown, Paula. The Chimbu. *A Study of Change in the New Guinea Highlands. 151 pp.*

Foner, N. Jamaica Farewell. *200 pp.*

Gudeman, Stephen. Relationships, Residence and the Individual. *A Rural Panamanian Community. 288 pp. 11 plates, 5 figures, 2 maps, 10 tables.*
The Demise of a Rural Economy. *From Subsistence to Capitalism in a Latin American Village. 160 pp.*

Hamnett, Ian. Chieftainship and Legitimacy. *An Anthropological Study of Executive Law in Lesotho. 163 pp.*

Hanson, F. Allan. Meaning in Culture. *127 pp.*

Hazan, H. The Limbo People. *A Study of the Constitution of the Time Universe Among the Aged. About 192 pp.*

Humphreys, S. C. Anthropology and the Greeks. *288 pp.*

Karp, I. Fields of Change Among the Iteso of Kenya. *140 pp.*

Lloyd, P. C. Power and Independence. *Urban Africans' Perception of Social Inequality. 264 pp.*

Parry, J. P. Caste and Kinship in Kangra. *352 pp. Illustrated.*

Pettigrew, Joyce. Robber Noblemen. *A Study of the Political System of the Sikh Jats. 284 pp.*

Street, Brian V. The Savage in Literature. *Representations of 'Primitive' Society in English Fiction, 1858–1920. 207 pp.*

Van Den Berghe, Pierre L. Power and Privilege at an African University. *278 pp.*

International Library of Phenomenology and Moral Sciences
General Editor John O'Neill

Apel, K.-O. Towards a Transformation of Philosophy. *308 pp.*

Bologh, R. W. Dialectical Phenomenology. *Marx's Method. 287 pp.*

Fekete, J. The Critical Twilight. *Explorations in the Ideology of Anglo-American Literary Theory from Eliot to McLuhan. 300 pp.*

Medina, A. Reflection, Time and the Novel. *Towards a Communicative Theory of Literature. 143 pp.*

International Library of Social Policy
General Editor Kathleen Jones

Bayley, M. Mental Handicap and Community Care. *426 pp.*

Bottoms, A. E. and McClean, J. D. Defendants in the Criminal Process. *284 pp.*

Bradshaw, J. The Family Fund. *An Initiative in Social Policy. About 224 pp.*

Butler, J. R. Family Doctors and Public Policy. *208 pp.*
Davies, Martin. Prisoners of Society. *Attitudes and Aftercare. 204 pp.*
Gittus, Elizabeth. Flats, Families and the Under-Fives. *285 pp.*
Holman, Robert. Trading in Children. *A Study of Private Fostering. 355 pp.*
Jeffs, A. Young People and the Youth Service. *160 pp.*
Jones, Howard and Cornes, Paul. Open Prisons. *288 pp.*
Jones, Kathleen. History of the Mental Health Service. *428 pp.*
Jones, Kathleen with **Brown, John, Cunningham, W. J., Roberts, Julian** and
    Williams, Peter. Opening the Door. *A Study of New Policies for the Mentally
    Handicapped. 278 pp.*
Karn, Valerie. Retiring to the Seaside. *400 pp. 2 maps. Numerous tables.*
King, R. D. and **Elliot, K. W.** Albany: Birth of a Prison—End of an Era. *394 pp.*
Thomas, J. E. The English Prison Officer since 1850: *A Study in Conflict. 258 pp.*
Walton, R. G. Women in Social Work. *303 pp.*
● **Woodward, J.** To Do the Sick No Harm. *A Study of the British Voluntary Hospital
    System to 1875. 234 pp.*

International Library of Welfare and Philosophy
General Editors Noel Timms and David Watson

● **McDermott, F. E.** (Ed.) Self-Determination in Social Work. *A Collection of Essays
    on Self-determination and Related Concepts by Philosophers and Social Work
    Theorists. Contributors: F. P. Biestek, S. Bernstein, A. Keith-Lucas, D. Sayer,
    H. H. Perelman, C. Whittington, R. F. Stalley, F. E. McDermott, I. Berlin, H. J.
    McCloskey, H. L. A. Hart, J. Wilson, A. I. Melden, S. I. Benn. 254 pp.*
● **Plant, Raymond.** Community and Ideology. *104 pp.*
Ragg, Nicholas M. People Not Cases. *A Philosophical Approach to Social Work.
    168 pp.*
● **Timms, Noel** and **Watson, David.** (Eds) Talking About Welfare. *Readings in
    Philosophy and Social Policy. Contributors: T. H. Marshall, R. B. Brandt, G. H.
    von Wright, K. Nielsen, M. Cranston, R. M. Titmuss, R. S. Downie, E. Telfer, D.
    Donnison, J. Benson, P. Leonard, A. Keith-Lucas, D. Walsh, I. T. Ramsey.
    320 pp.*
● Philosophy in Social Work. *250 pp.*
● **Weale, A.** Equality and Social Policy. *164 pp.*

Library of Social Work
General Editor Noel Timms

● **Baldock, Peter.** Community Work and Social Work. *140 pp.*
○ **Beedell, Christopher.** Residential Life with Children. *210 pp. Crown 8vo.*
● **Berry, Juliet.** Daily Experience in Residential Life. *A Study of Children and their
    Care-givers. 202 pp.*
○ Social Work with Children. *190 pp. Crown 8vo.*
● **Brearley, C. Paul.** Residential Work with the Elderly. *116 pp.*
● Social Work, Ageing and Society. *126 pp.*
● **Cheetham, Juliet.** Social Work with Immigrants. *240 pp. Crown 8vo.*
● **Cross, Crispin P.** (Ed.) Interviewing and Communication in Social Work.
    *Contributions by C. P. Cross, D. Laurenson, B. Strutt, S. Raven. 192 pp. Crown
    8vo.*

- **Curnock, Kathleen** and **Hardiker, Pauline.** Towards Practice Theory. *Skills and Methods in Social Assessments. 208 pp.*
- **Davies, Bernard.** The Use of Groups in Social Work Practice. *158 pp.*
- **Davies, Martin.** Support Systems in Social Work. *144 pp.*
- **Ellis, June.** (Ed.) West African Families in Britain. *A Meeting of Two Cultures. Contributions by Pat Stapleton, Vivien Biggs. 150 pp. 1 Map.*
- **Hart, John.** Social Work and Sexual Conduct. *230 pp.*
- **Hutten, Joan M.** Short-Term Contracts in Social Work. *Contributions by Stella M. Hall, Elsie Osborne, Mannie Sher, Eva Sternberg, Elizabeth Tuters. 134 pp.*
- **Jackson, Michael P.** and **Valencia, B. Michael.** Financial Aid Through Social Work. *140 pp.*
- **Jones, Howard.** The Residential Community. *A Setting for Social Work. 150 pp.*
- (Ed.) Towards a New Social Work. *Contributions by Howard Jones, D. A. Fowler, J. R. Cypher, R. G. Walton, Geoffrey Mungham, Philip Priestley, Ian Shaw, M. Bartley, R. Deacon, Irwin Epstein, Geoffrey Pearson. 184 pp.*
- **Jones, Ray** and **Pritchard, Colin.** (Eds) Social Work With Adolescents. *Contributions by Ray Jones, Colin Pritchard, Jack Dunham, Florence Rossetti, Andrew Kerslake, John Burns, William Gregory, Graham Templeman, Kenneth E. Reid, Audrey Taylor. About 170 pp.*
- ○ **Jordon, William.** The Social Worker in Family Situations. *160 pp. Crown 8vo.*
- **Laycock, A. L.** Adolescents and Social Work. *128 pp. Crown 8vo.*
- **Lees, Ray.** Politics and Social Work. *128 pp. Crown 8vo.*
- Research Strategies for Social Welfare. *112 pp. Tables.*
- ○ **McCullough, M. K.** and **Ely, Peter J.** Social Work with Groups. *127 pp. Crown 8vo.*
- **Moffett, Jonathan.** Concepts in Casework Treatment. *128 pp. Crown 8vo.*
- **Parsloe, Phyllida.** Juvenile Justice in Britain and the United States. *The Balance of Needs and Rights. 336 pp.*
- **Plant, Raymond.** Social and Moral Theory in Casework. *112 pp. Crown 8vo.*
- **Priestley, Philip, Fears, Denise** and **Fuller, Roger.** Justice for Juveniles. *The 1969 Children and Young Persons Act: A Case for Reform? 128 pp.*
- **Pritchard, Colin** and **Taylor, Richard.** Social Work: Reform or Revolution? *170 pp.*
- ○ **Pugh, Elisabeth.** Social Work in Child Care. *128 pp. Crown 8vo.*
- **Robinson, Margaret.** Schools and Social Work. *282 pp.*
- ○ **Ruddock, Ralph.** Roles and Relationships. *128 pp. Crown 8vo.*
- **Sainsbury, Eric.** Social Diagnosis in Casework. *118 pp. Crown 8vo.*
- Social Work with Families. *Perceptions of Social Casework among Clients of a Family Service. 188 pp.*
- **Seed, Philip.** The Expansion of Social Work in Britain. *128 pp. Crown 8vo.*
- **Shaw, John.** The Self in Social Work. *124 pp.*
- **Smale, Gerald G.** Prophecy, Behaviour and Change. *An Examination of Self-fulfilling Prophecies in Helping Relationships. 116 pp. Crown 8vo.*
- **Smith, Gilbert.** Social Need. *Policy, Practice and Research. 155 pp.*
- Social Work and the Sociology of Organisations. *124 pp. Revised edition.*
- **Sutton, Carole.** Psychology for Social Workers and Counsellors. *An Introduction. 248 pp.*
- **Timms, Noel.** Language of Social Casework. *122 pp. Crown 8vo.*
- Recording in Social Work. *124 pp. Crown 8vo.*
- **Todd, F. Joan.** Social Work with the Mentally Subnormal. *96 pp. Crown 8vo.*
- **Walrond-Skinner, Sue.** Family Therapy. *The Treatment of Natural Systems. 172 pp.*
- **Warham, Joyce.** An Introduction to Administration for Social Workers. *Revised edition. 112 pp.*
- An Open Case. *The Organisational Context of Social Work. 172 pp.*
- ○ **Wittenberg, Isca Salzberger.** Psycho-Analytic Insight and Relationships. *A Kleinian Approach. 196 pp. Crown 8vo.*

12

Primary Socialization, Language and Education
General Editor Basil Bernstein

Adlam, Diana S., *with the assistance of Geoffrey Turner and Lesley Lineker.* Code in Context. *272 pp.*
Bernstein, Basil. Class, Codes and Control. *3 volumes.*
● 1. *Theoretical Studies Towards a Sociology of Language. 254 pp.*
2. *Applied Studies Towards a Sociology of Language. 377 pp.*
● 3. *Towards a Theory of Educational Transmission. 167 pp.*
Brandis, W. and **Bernstein, B.** Selection and Control. *176 pp.*
Brandis, Walter and **Henderson, Dorothy.** Social Class, Language and Communication. *288 pp.*
Cook-Gumperz, Jenny. Social Control and Socialization. *A Study of Class Differences in the Language of Maternal Control. 290 pp.*
● **Gahagan, D. M.** and **G. A.** Talk Reform. *Exploration in Language for Infant School Children. 160 pp.*
Hawkins, P. R. Social Class, the Nominal Group and Verbal Strategies. *About 220 pp.*
Robinson, W. P. and **Rackstraw, Susan D. A.** A Question of Answers. *2 volumes. 192 pp. and 180 pp.*
Turner, Geoffrey J. and **Mohan, Bernard A.** A Linguistic Description and Computer Programme for Children's Speech. *208 pp.*

Reports of the Institute of Community Studies

Baker, J. The Neighbourhood Advice Centre. A Community Project in Camden. *320 pp.*
● **Cartwright, Ann.** Patients and their Doctors. *A Study of General Practice. 304 pp.*
Dench, Geoff. Maltese in London. *A Case-study in the Erosion of Ethnic Consciousness. 302 pp.*
Jackson, Brian and **Marsden, Dennis.** Education and the Working Class: *Some General Themes Raised by a Study of 88 Working-class Children in a Northern Industrial City. 268 pp. 2 folders.*
Marris, Peter. The Experience of Higher Education. *232 pp. 27 tables.*
● Loss and Change. *192 pp.*
Marris, Peter and **Rein, Martin.** Dilemmas of Social Reform. *Poverty and Community Action in the United States. 256 pp.*
Marris, Peter and **Somerset, Anthony.** African Businessmen. *A Study of Entrepreneurship and Development in Kenya. 256 pp.*
Mills, Richard. Young Outsiders: *a Study in Alternative Communities. 216 pp.*
Runciman, W. G. Relative Deprivation and Social Justice. *A Study of Attitudes to Social Inequality in Twentieth-Century England. 352 pp.*
Willmott, Peter. Adolescent Boys in East London. *230 pp.*
Willmott, Peter and **Young, Michael.** Family and Class in a London Suburb. *202 pp. 47 tables.*
Young, Michael and **McGeeney, Patrick.** Learning Begins at Home. *A Study of a Junior School and its Parents. 128 pp.*
Young, Michael and **Willmott, Peter.** Family and Kinship in East London. *Foreword by Richard M. Titmuss. 252 pp. 39 tables.*
The Symmetrical Family. *410 pp.*

Reports of the Institute for Social Studies in Medical Care

Cartwright, Ann, Hockey, Lisbeth and Anderson, John J. Life Before Death. *310 pp.*
Dunnell, Karen and Cartwright, Ann. Medicine Takers, Prescribers and Hoarders. *190 pp.*
Farrell, C. My Mother Said. . . *A Study of the Way Young People Learned About Sex and Birth Control. 288 pp.*

Medicine, Illness and Society
General Editor W. M. Williams

Hall, David J. Social Relations & Innovation. *Changing the State of Play in Hospitals. 232 pp.*
Hall, David J. and Stacey, M. (Eds) Beyond Separation. *234 pp.*
Robinson, David. The Process of Becoming Ill. *142 pp.*
Stacey, Margaret *et al.* Hospitals, Children and Their Families. *The Report of a Pilot Study. 202 pp.*
Stimson, G. V. and Webb, B. Going to See the Doctor. *The Consultation Process in General Practice. 155 pp.*

Monographs in Social Theory
General Editor Arthur Brittan

● Barnes, B. Scientific Knowledge and Sociological Theory. *192 pp.*
Bauman, Zygmunt. Culture as Praxis. *204 pp.*
● Dixon, Keith. Sociological Theory. *Pretence and Possibility. 142 pp.*
The Sociology of Belief. *Fallacy and Foundation. About 160 pp.*
Goff, T. W. Marx and Mead. *Contributions to a Sociology of Knowledge. 176 pp.*
Meltzer, B. N., Petras, J. W. and Reynolds, L. T. Symbolic Interactionism. *Genesis, Varieties and Criticisms. 144 pp.*
● Smith, Anthony D. The Concept of Social Change. *A Critique of the Functionalist Theory of Social Change. 208 pp.*

Routledge Social Science Journals

The British Journal of Sociology. *Editor – Angus Stewart; Associate Editor – Leslie Sklair. Vol. 1, No. 1 – March 1950 and Quarterly. Roy. 8vo. All back issues available. An international journal publishing original papers in the field of sociology and related areas.*
Community Work. *Edited by David Jones and Marjorie Mayo. 1973. Published annually.*
Economy and Society. *Vol. 1, No. 1. February 1972 and Quarterly. Metric Roy. 8vo. A journal for all social scientists covering sociology, philosophy, anthropology, economics and history. All back numbers available.*

Ethnic and Racial Studies. *Editor – John Stone. Vol. 1 – 1978. Published quarterly.*
Religion. Journal of Religion and Religions. *Chairman of Editorial Board, Ninian Smart. Vol. 1, No. 1, Spring 1971. A journal with an inter-disciplinary approach to the study of the phenomena of religion. All back numbers available.*
Sociology of Health and Illness. *A Journal of Medical Sociology. Editor – Alan Davies; Associate Editor – Ray Jobling. Vol. 1, Spring 1979. Published 3 times per annum.*
Year Book of Social Policy in Britain. *Edited by Kathleen Jones. 1971. Published annually.*

Social and Psychological Aspects of Medical Practice

Editor   Trevor Silverstone

Lader, Malcolm. Psychophysiology of Mental Illness. *280 pp.*
● **Silverstone, Trevor** and **Turner, Paul.** Drug Treatment in Psychiatry. *Revised edition. 256 pp.*
Whiteley, J. S. and **Gordon, J.** Group Approaches in Psychiatry. *240 pp.*

Printed and bound in Great Britain by
Redwood Burn Limited, Trowbridge & Esher